P9-CQZ-475

TAKE AN INTIMATE PEEK AT THE REAL WOMAN BEHIND THE GOLDEN VOICE . . .

BARBRA STREISAND: *The Untold Story*

She is an EVERGREEN . . .

She is a mega-star and a living legend who has been capturing audiences for thirty years. Her Las Vegas comeback, and her triumphant international concert tour have made her more popular than ever . . .

Share her MEMORIES . . .

Her lonely childhood in Brooklyn, the shattering loss of her father, and her determination to become a star . . .

She is THE GREATEST STAR . . .

How she became an Oscar-winning movie star, the leading lady to movie heroes from Robert Redford to Nick Nolte, and her off-screen romances with Ryan O'Neal, Warren Beatty, Don Johnson, Andre Agassi, and more . . .

SINS AND SCANDALS!
GO BEHIND THE SCENES WITH PINNACLE

JULIA: THE UNTOLD STORY OF AMERICA'S
PRETTY WOMAN   (898, $4.99)
by Eileen Joyce
She lit up the screen in STEEL MAGNOLIAS and PRETTY
WOMAN. She's been paired with scores of stunning leading men.
And now, here's an explosive unauthorized biography of Julia
Roberts that tells all. Read about Julia's recent surprise marriage to
Lyle Lovitt—Her controversial two-year disappearance—Her big
comeback that has Tinseltown talking—and much, much more!

SEAN CONNERY: FROM 007 TO
HOLLYWOOD ICON   (742, $4.50)
by Andrew Rule
After nearly thirty years—and countless films—Sean Connery is
still one of the most irresistible and bankable stars in Hollywood.
Now, for the first time, go behind the scenes to meet the man behind the suave 007 myth. From his beginnings in a Scotland slum
to international stardom, take an intimate look at this most fascinating and exciting superstar.

HOWARD STERN: BIG MOUTH   (796, $4.99)
by Jeff Menell
Brilliant, stupid, sexist, racist, obscene, hilarious—and just plain
gross! Howard Stern is the man you love to hate. Now you can find
out the real story behind morning radio's number one bad boy!

THE "I HATE BRENDA" BOOK   (797, $4.50)
By Michael Carr & Darby
From the editors of the official "I HATE BRENDA" newsletter
comes everything you ever wanted to know about Shannen Do-
herty. Here's the dirt on a young woman who seems to be careening
through the heady galaxy of Hollywood, a burning asteroid spin-
ning "out of control!"

THE RICHEST GIRL IN THE WORLD   (792, $4.99)
by Stephanie Mansfield
At the age of thirteen, Doris Duke inherited a $100 million tobacco
fortune. By the time she was thirty, Doris Duke had lavished millions on her lovers and husbands. An eccentric who thumbed her
nose at society, Duke's circle of friends included Jackie Onassis,
Macolm Forbes, Truman Capote, Andy Warhol and Imelda Mar-
cos. But all the money in the world couldn't buy the love that she
searched for!

*Available wherever paperbacks are sold, or order direct from the
Publisher. Send cover price plus 50¢ per copy for mailing and handling to Penguin USA, P.O. Box 999, c/o Dept. 17109, Bergen-
field, NJ 07621. Residents of New York and Tennessee must
include sales tax. DO NOT SEND CASH.*

BARBRA STREISAND
—The Untold Story—

NELLIE BLY

PINNACLE BOOKS
WINDSOR PUBLISHING CORP.

PINNACLE BOOKS are published by

Windsor Publishing Corp.
850 Third Avenue
New York, NY 10022

Copyright © 1994 by Sarah Gallick

All rights reserved. No part of this book may be reproduced in any form or by any means without the prior written consent of the Publisher, excepting brief quotes used in reviews.

If you purchased this book without a cover, you should be aware that this book is stolen property. It was reported as "unsold and destroyed" to the Publisher and neither the Author nor the Publisher has received any payment for this "stripped book."

The P logo Reg U.S. Pat. & TM Off. Pinnacle is a trademark of Windsor Publishing Corp.

First Pinnacle Printing: September, 1994

Printed in the United States of America

This book is for Walter Zacharius because he asked for it. I would also like to thank the Kensington-Zebra-Pinnacle team, especially Tracy Bernstein, Joyce Kaplan, Suzanne Henry, Amy Stecher, Mike Capobianco, and Kevin Bohan. Special thanks to Julie Stone and Susan Lippe for their work on the photo section and to Marc Cerasini for his invaluable research.

I also have boundless gratitude to Sarah Gallick, without whom I would not exist, and to Michael V. Clark for making that existence worthwhile.

TABLE OF CONTENTS

Prologue

Washington, D.C.
January 1993

The greatest female star in American history took the stage to salute her president. Rumors that she had refused to perform at Bill Clinton's inaugural gala unless she was permitted to introduce the new president were forgotten as she launched into a rare public performance. At 51 she had never looked better, her voluptuous decolletage and long slim legs displayed to advantage in a Donna Karan design that would later be described in the *New York Times* as her "peekaboo-power suit."

They had much to celebrate, Bill Clinton and Barbra Streisand, the Baptist-born Rhodes Scholar from Arkansas and the performer-philanthropist from Hollywood by way of a Brooklyn yeshiva and Erasmus Hall high school. Both shared a deep commitment to the Democratic party, liberal values, and a drive to improve the world.

But more than that, they shared fundamental life-forming experiences. Clinton's father died just weeks before he was born; Barbra's father passed away when she was barely fifteen months old. They had grown up poor, had known what it was like to be at the mercy of an abusive, overbearing stepfather. Each of them had looked for father-figures in other powerful men who helped them at key moments in their career.

And each of them also shared a powerful attraction to the opposite sex.

That feminine allure has always been one of the most fascinating things about Barbra Streisand. A formidable talent but never a conventional beauty, Barbra has managed to fascinate not just the general public, but some of the most powerful men in the world. Bill Clinton is not the first head of state to be in her thrall.

Her lovers have included internationally famous leading men and powerful industry moguls. Her advisors, like Ray Stark who cast her in *Funny Girl,* and Marty Erlichman, who has served as her personal manager throughout most of her career, quickly learned that the way to treat Barbra was as an equal.

She is both a woman of passion and a woman of business, a woman who could give her whole heart and soul to a relationship—as she did with her first and only husband, Elliott Gould—and yet she is also a woman who has shrewdly profited personally and professionally from every romantic relationship she has ever had.

Here at last is the story of Barbra Streisand, the woman, and the men in her life.

One

The Two Men Who Left Her

"When a kid grows up missing one parent there's a big gap that has to be filled. It's like someone being blind, they hear better. With me, I tell more, I sensed more, I wanted more, you know, and it left me open to life."

—Barbra

The first man in Barbra Streisand's life, her father, left her when she was fifteen months old. As a child, she barely remembered him, but what she would remember forever was the yawning, painful gap that the death of Manny Streisand left in her life.

Emanuel Streisand was the son of an immigrant fishmonger. He was handsome, healthy, and fiercely ambitious. He earned a master's degree in education at Columbia University and taught English literature at the George Westinghouse Vocational High School in Brooklyn. He was an athlete as well as a scholar, a big, strong man with big and exciting dreams for himself, his wife, Diana Rosen, and their small family.

He planned his life with great attention to detail. He and Diana had been marked forever by the Great Depression.

Raised in the insular immigrant communities of Brooklyn, they courted for years before they married in 1930. They waited for five years to have their first child, a son, Sheldon, and another eight years to have their second, a daughter they named Barbara Joan.

Neither Barbra nor her mother, both usually very candid, has ever discussed why these names were chosen. Yet it's worth noting that the year Barbra was born, two of the top box office stars were Brooklyn-born Barbara Stanwyck and Joan Crawford. Both these actresses had long careers, played strong-willed women in their films, and were equally strong-willed off-screen. Even if the names are an unlikely coincidence, it seems somehow fitting that Barbra Joan Streisand should follow in their career footsteps—a strong-willed woman in charge of her destiny.

But that would come later. First came the difficult childhood years.

When Barbara Joan was born on April 24, 1942, Diana was 33 and Manny was 34. They had every reason to believe that their lives were proceeding perfectly according to plan. It would not be long before they could move to a bigger place, maybe even a house in the suburbs. They wanted to give their children the advantages they never had. But that was not to be. Life had a way of messing up their plans. A terrible way. And the bright promise that beckoned to Diana and Manny and their children was not to be. At least not for a long time.

It was traditional for Jewish families of New York's Lower East Side, Brooklyn, and the Bronx to seek refuge from the summer heat in the Catskill Mountains of upstate New York. Around those rich, green mountains grew a great resort area that included the fabled Concord and Grossinger hotels as well as modest bungalow colonies. Parents who could not afford to take time off themselves could at least send their children to camps in the Catskills. If especially lucky, they had a sports-minded father like Manny Streisand, who got work in such a camp the summer of 1943 and could bring along his wife and children.

In 1943 Manny Streisand was a strapping young man who went to work as head counselor at a friend's summer camp, Camp Cascade in upstate New York. Besides the extra money he would earn it meant a chance to bring his wife and family up to benefit from the fresh air and rustic atmosphere of the scenic Catskills.

But Manny Streisand, 34, never made it back to Brooklyn that summer. Diana always told Barbra that he had died that August 3 of a cerebral hemorrhage brought on by overwork, something that would leave Barbra dreading that the same fate awaited her. "I thought I might die of overwork too," Barbra recalls.

Finally, when Barbra was a grown woman, Diana told her the truth: Manny Streisand had died of respiratory failure probably induced when morphine was injected into his neck to halt an epileptic seizure.

Manny Streisand and his bright promise of the future were gone. Diana Streisand was a bereaved widow with two young children and Barbara Joan, only fifteen months old, was marked forever.

"I always felt I never had a father," Barbra has said. "There wasn't even a picture of us together. Only his books down in the cellar, tied up with string." If Barbra thought about Manny at all, it was to resent him for making her "the only kid on the block without a father."

From the very beginning, the sudden loss of her father left Barbra feeling like an outsider. Forever after, she would be seeking that lost father in the men in her life.

The loss of her father was heightened by what Barbra considered an emotional abandonment by her mother. Diana Streisand's mind was on basic survival. Manny's death had left her destitute and she had to leave the apartment on Schenectady Avenue and move back in with her parents on Pulaski Street in the always modest and now rapidly declining area of Brooklyn known as Bedford-Stuyvesant.

It was not a happy home. Barbra's brother Sheldon recalls that his grandparents were "decent, hard-working people, but there was no love in that house. I remember there was a huge table in the dining room and Barbra and I would scuttle under it to avoid beatings."

Barbra, too, has few fond memories of these years. "From the day I was born," she says, "I was trying to get out. I've never been nostalgic about my past."

Diana worked all day, and had rather retro ideas about childrearing. "Spanking," she proudly recommended. "It saves the psychiatrist's fees. There's a Jewish saying that whenever a child gets spanked, it finally finds its way to the head so the head clears."

Diana had little time for compliments or building her daughter's self-esteem. "Never give your kids too much praise," she advises. "In fact, I try to tone them down if I see they have an exaggerated opinion of themselves. I just kind of make a remark that calms them down."

At four, little Barbra was sent to kindergarten at a nearby yeshiva which she attended up to third grade. Barbra was the class clown. "When the rabbi would go out of the room I'd yell 'Christmas! Christmas!'—a bad word for a Hebrew school," she recalls. "But even I couldn't bring myself to cross my fingers." When school was out, Barbra would visit the apartment of her friend Irving whose parents had a 7 1/2 inch television set. "I remember his mother cooking stuffed cabbage and knitting every afternoon, while we watched Laurel and Hardy through a magnifying window."

Her other best friends were an atheist and a Catholic. Barbra was fascinated with Catholics, the nuns, the priests, their habits and rituals. Like her Catholic friend, she would greet the parish priest with a curtsy and a "Hello, Father." It's easy to imagine the magical power of the word "father" on a girl who had lost her own father before the age of two.

When Barbra was five, Diana, concerned about her daughter's anemia, sent her to a Jewish health camp in the Catskills. It was not a happy experience. "I remember their taking off my clothes and dumping me into this bath like I was a piece of dirt. They scrubbed me and washed me and put this lice disinfectant in my hair, then they put me into their uniform." Barbra felt more comfortable with the older campers. She befriended a camper named Maria. "I remember jumping into a pool of water where I thought I was going to drown and [Maria] pulled me out. So I'm afraid of water today."

For years afterward, Barbra would have asthma attacks whenever she went to the country. She would blame them on her associations with the camp. "My association went back to when I was five years old at health camp. I was homesick. Every day I would cry and the kids would make fun of me. I would say, 'I'm not crying, I have a loose tear duct that just runs.' My possession, my identity, my sense of self was only around my maroon sweater with wooden buttons that Toby Berakow, the lady who took care of me during the day while my mother went to work, knitted for me."

In 1949, at age seven, she was sent to health camp again. And when Diana came to visit, she brought an unpleasant surprise: her new suitor, Louis Kind.

Chances are that no man could have replaced Manny Streisand in his daughter's heart and mind. By the time Barbra was seven, she had idealized him. Poor Louis Kind never had a chance.

"When my mother came to visit me with my future stepfather, Louis Kind, I said, 'You're not leaving without me. I am not staying here any longer.' I was always able to manipulate my mother. I made her pack my bags and she took me home. With Louis Kind in the car. He hated me ever since. I mean, until he died. He was allergic to kids, as my mother said—even though I must have been pretty obnoxious."

At 55 Louis Kind was fourteen years older than Diana, and had plied a variety of trades including real estate sales, used car sales, and tailoring. Louis and Barbra clashed from the beginning, but Diana prevailed: she married him and together the family left the declining streets of Bedford-Stuyvesant for a cozy, if banal, two-bedroom apartment on Newkirk and Van Nostrand Avenues in middle-class Flatbush. Barbra's new school, P.S. 89, was across the street.

The first night in the new apartment Barbra insisted on sleeping in the bed with her mother. When she woke up the next morning, she had developed strange clicks in her ears. Her mother dismissed Barbra's complaints, but the clicks did not go away. In fact, according to Barbra, a few years later she developed a strange high-pitched noise that sounded continuously in her ears. This condition, later diagnosed as tinnitus, would plague her for the rest of her life.

For a time, at least, Louis Kind was a good provider and Diana was able to stop working and stay at home with the children. Barbra was enrolled in Miss Marsh's Dance School for ballet lessons, "fantasizing about being a ballerina, just walking around the house in toe shoes." But the family still lived modestly and Barbra slept on the living room couch. Barbra claims that in all those years Louis Kind never talked to her, except to tell her to be quiet.

Her brother Sheldon confirms Barbra's memories of their stepfather: "He taunted her continually, telling her how plain she was compared to Roslyn, her little sister, who was his daughter with my mother."

Certainly Louis Kind was not a kind or generous man, especially not after Diana gave birth to his own daughter,

Roslyn, a year after their marriage. Barbra put it simply: "He disliked me."

At nine, she was miserable, lonely, and friendless. "What did I do?" she would ask plaintively. "What did I vibrate? What made them angry at me?"

"We didn't have fun when I was growing up," she says now. "I was never taken anywhere."

Around this time, Barbra discovered a pamphlet about cancer and began to fear that she had all the symptoms and was going to die.

Sometimes she would try to imagine her future, but she couldn't. "There was a blank screen, no husband, no children, no nothing. I decided that meant I was going to die—I wasn't being melodramatic or anything, I really believed it, and I would think 'That's too bad, because I really could have done things.' "

But by now, Barbra had discovered that she loved to sing, that she liked the sound and that other people liked it too. Whether imitating Johnny Mathis in the halls of her apartment house because they rang like a concert hall, until the super threw her out, or singing along to Joni James records, she came to life when she sang. And people paid attention. The way a father would. The way Manny Streisand would have if he had lived. The way her stepfather Louis Kind should have, but didn't.

Diana had inherited her own beautiful voice from her cantor father, but she regarded her daughter's gift with trepidation. She accompanied little Barbra to auditions for shows in Manhattan, but no jobs resulted.

"I was kind of a loner, a real ugly kid, the kind who looks ridiculous with a ribbon in her hair. And skinny."

"I love my mother," Barbra has said on more than one occasion, "but I used to resent her for never encouraging my acting ambitions. She wanted me to be a school clerk—all those paid vacations." According to Barbra, Diana always told her that she was too thin, too unattractive, too peculiar to become a movie star.

Yet, Barbra acknowledges that Diana's attitude probably had something to do with her success, because she was always trying to prove to her mother that she was worthwhile, that she wasn't just another skinny *marink*.

"My mother egged me on. The more she said I'd never make it, that I was too skinny, the more determined I got," says Barbra.

Diana urged her to study typing and stenography, "just in case." But, as Barbra explains: "I knew I had talent and I was afraid that if I learned to type I would become a secretary."

At eleven, Barbra discovered another talent: like her namesakes, Barbara Stanwyck and Joan Crawford, little Barbara Joan Streisand could act up a storm. When her mother once slapped her for misbehaving, Barbra pretended she was deaf for four hours and Diana believed her.

By 1953 Diana's marriage to Louis Kind had begun to show signs of strain and by 1956 Kind had departed for parts unknown. Diana and Roslyn may have missed him, but Barbra could only have been relieved.

By that time, she was babysitting for neighbors who owned a restaurant, Choy's Chinese. Just the way she would one day learn all the jobs involved in making a movie or a record album, Barbra soon learned all the jobs at the restaurant. She was working the cash register and filling in as hostess and taking orders over the telephone or waiting on tables. She became a member of the family, even picking up a few words of Chinese and a lifelong taste for Chinese food.

Muriel Choy, the matriarch of the family, was Barbra's confidante, talking about life and love and sex. At home, Barbra did not fit in at all.

"I used to say, O.K., Ma, did you find me on a doorstep or what?"

"My grandmother used to call me *'farbrent,'* which means 'on fire.' I just couldn't accept no for an answer. I still can't."

"I was a peculiar kid," Barbra admits. "I had things on my mind." What kind of things? "My ambitions to be, ah, you know, an actress."

It's ironic, given Diana's resistance to Barbra's career, that the star freely admits "My voice came from my mother."

In fact, Diana was responsible for Barbra's first recording—when she was thirteen!

The summer of 1955, Diana took Barbra and little sister Roz to the Catskills for a vacation. While there they met a piano player who encouraged Barbra to make her first recording the following December. It was a little 45 rpm demo recorded at the Nola Recording Studios on December 29, 1955, with only the piano player as her accompanist. Diana sang "One Kiss" and another operetta piece, then Barbra sang "You'll Never Know" and "Zing! Went the Strings of My Heart!" "I still have the record," Barbra told an interviewer ten years later, "I even improvised at the end."

Barbra had already entered high school that September. Erasmus Hall was then one of the finest public high schools in New York City and its notable graduates include her namesake Barbara Stanwyck and her future duet partner Neil Diamond. Although in early interviews Barbra liked to paint a portrait of herself as a lonely, excluded outsider, the fact is that Barbra was part of the scene. If not the most popular, or recognized as the most talented, she was surrounded by friends and was an active member of the chorus and Choral Club.

What friends remember about her from those days were her careful attention to make-up, her voice, her fastidious approach to clothes, her beautiful hands, and long nails. Barbra claims she grew her nails long so no one would dare ask her to type.

What Barbra remembers about her high school years is her crush on chess champion Bobby Fischer. He was a year behind her in school, but they would have lunch together every day and he would concentrate on reading *Mad* magazine which he seemed to find much more interesting than Barbra.

"When a kid grows up missing one parent there's a big gap that has to be filled. It's like someone being blind, they hear better. With me, I tell more, I sensed more, I wanted more, you know, and it left me open to life."

Young Barbra sought escape at the Loew's Kings Theatre on Flatbush Avenue where she watched life as it ought to be—on the big screen.

"They had the best ice cream. . . . I always loved the smell of that theater, the cooled refrigeration and the hot buttered popcorn and they had the best Mello-rolls. Whatever happened to Mello-rolls? . . . How beautiful it all looked, how perfect it all was, until I stepped one foot out of the theater, and it all seemed so depressing. Inside, I was the character in the movie, not the actress. I was not Vivien Leigh, I was Scarlett O'Hara, and I loved being the most beautiful woman kissed by the beautiful man."

It was at Loew's that she first fell in love with Marlon Brando, a man she idolized as a man and as an actor, on screen in *Guys and Dolls*. But Barbra insists she never had any musical idols. "My favorite singer while I was growing up was Johnny Mathis. I also listened a lot to Joni James records." While other kids were imitating Elvis Presley, Barbra was listening to Johnny Mathis, modeling her style after his. Practicing her singing style in the halls of her apartment building, because they rang like a concert hall, until the super threw her out.

It was also in high school that Barbra first began to feel

the pull between singing and acting. She knew she was a good singer; she wanted to be a great actress.

"When I was thirteen years old, a group of us auditioned for a radio show as actresses," she recalls. "I did a speech from Saint Joan—'He who tells the truth shall surely be caught.' "

Barbra was fourteen when she saw her first Broadway play, *The Diary of Anne Frank,* at the Cort Theatre. "I was sitting way up high in the balcony. I was awfully disappointed, looking at the dreary setting. The only thing I knew was movies with all the glamour and everything."

In 1957, the summer of her sophomore year, stagestruck Barbra lied about her age, claiming to be seventeen, and took a job as a summer apprentice at the Malden Bridge Playhouse in the Adirondacks in upstate New York, with one hundred and fifty dollars her mother had given her. "Later I found it was really money my grandfather had left me. At the last minute it was a question of using the money for summer stock or to fix my teeth."

Barbra had gone to the dentist and he had discovered that she still had her baby teeth on each side, and the other ones had never come down. "He pulled one on each side, then wanted to pull two more and give me braces, but I wouldn't let him. For the next year I went around with these holes on both sides of my mouth. Imagine an actress without her teeth! I used Aspergum—it was the closest color I could get to real teeth. I would press a piece in each side of my mouth, like false teeth. Sometimes it would drop out of one side or the other so I looked like a nut."

In spite of her dental problems, Barbra had a wonderful time at the playhouse and returned to New York with an Actor's Equity card.

She was cast as Millie Owens, the sixteen-year-old Kansas tomboy in *Picnic,* and as Elsa, the sexy secretary in *Desk Set,* and she was good enough to be invited back the following season.

In her bestselling autobiography *Enter Talking,* Joan Rivers recalls meeting the very young, very ambitious Barbra Streisand around that time. An actor friend brought her to the Armand de Beauchamp School of the Theater, located six flights up in a West Seventies brownstone, which was mounting an off-Broadway showcase of a play called *Seawood.* Joan believes that her main qualification for being cast was her assurance that she had a lot of relatives in the metropolitan area who were sure to buy tickets.

Rivers recalls Barbra as "a skinny high school girl with a large nose and a pin that said, 'Go Erasmus.'" Rivers was cast as "The Woman in Black" which had been written as "The Man in Black" when Ralph Meaker played the role in Chicago. To get the part, she convinced Armand that the character could be played as a lesbian.

During rehearsals in Armand's apartment, the cast sat around and talked show business in the kitchen.

"I liked the high school girl with the big nose who was funny and made jokes," Rivers says. "We had immediate rapport, maybe because she seemed a tough little hustler, paying her way by working part time as a cashier at a Chinese restaurant, but still obviously vulnerable. . . . Despite being the youngest person by far, she was very outgoing and at the first rehearsal came right over to me and said, "Hi, what's your name? My name's Barbra Streisand."

"Even then she clearly intended to become Barbra Streisand. She was impressive, carrying at her age a full theatrical makeup kit with grease paint in *tubes* and an Equity card earned in summer stock. Even though she was incongruous among us, so young with her Brooklyn accent, she was obviously very serious about acting and we felt a force inside her, an authenticity even in the midst of the idiocy of *Seawood.*"

They rehearsed in the heatless apartment for two weeks, sipping hot coffee in the kitchen between scenes to keep warm.

Opening night, the Garret Theatre itself was in the attic above Armand's apartment, reached by a narrow, rickety flight of stairs from his living room.

Joan's role required her to make love to Barbra, or rather her character, "Lorna of the Dunes." "The actual performance is a blur—the mind protects itself," Rivers says. "I do remember I had a big love scene where I told Barbra I loved her very much and she rejected me and I had a knife in my hand and tried to kill her and then myself. I also remember a horrendous lot of coughing, like a tubercular ward, and knowing this whole thing was insane and wanting to turn and wink at the audience, sitting there in overcoats. But I felt fine performing, did not feel ashamed, and thought I was not bad as a woman in love with Barbra Streisand."

The next day's review in *Show Business* called *Seawood* sophomoric, soap opera-ish, and ridiculous—and said the performances couldn't be evaluated because the material was so bad.

Six weeks into their run, Joan arrived at Armand's door only to be told that the play had closed. She got her costume and make-up and on the way down the stairs ran into Barbra coming up. "It's closed. There's no play," she told her. Barbra shrugged. "That's just as well. I got midterms."

Two

The Boys in the Bars

"Streisand, whether she likes it or not, became the mother of a post-Garland show-biz phenomenon: the pop diva whose career is launched largely by gay male audiences."

—Kevin Sessums

The first fifteen years of Barbra's life were dominated by two men who weren't there: her lost father Manny and her distant stepfather Louis Kind. It was in high school that she discovered a circle of young men who shared her interests in the arts, her restlessness, her loathing for the conventional: the boys of Greenwich Village.

Barbra started travelling into Manhattan on the subway with friends and began to make new friends among the artistic young men who made their homes in the Village. These relationships would have a tremendous effect on Barbra. Not being interested in her sexually, they could see past the awkward, plain-faced girl with the Flatbush accent and they could see her potential. Over the next five years, some of them would help mold Barbra Joan Streisand from Newkirk Avenue into Barbra Streisand—International Superstar. Even more would pack the small Village clubs where she got her start as a performer.

Those who remember Barbra from this time recall a girl who was "always late, very intense, wearing a coat of some immense plaid and eating yogurt."

She never doubted her talent. "I knew I was good, but no one would let me read until I had experience, so how could I get experience? Besides, I wasn't the ingenue type those casting creeps were looking for. I could have changed the way I looked, had my nose fixed or something, but I just wouldn't. That wouldn't have been honest, right?"

Barbra graduated from Erasmus in January, 1959, not yet sixteen, and announced she was moving to Manhattan. Sometimes she shared apartments, more often she carried a cot around with her and slept wherever she could—in friends' apartments, public relations offices, studio lofts. For a while she swept out the Cherry Lane Theatre where she met acting coach Alan Miller and his wife.

Miller agreed to coach Barbra in exchange for babysitting his son. At the same time, she was studying with another coach, Eli Rill, under the name Angelina Scarangella, so he wouldn't know she was studying with anyone else.

Through the Millers, Barbra was exposed to a whole new world. She went along as babysitter when they spent the summer of 1959 at the Clinton Playhouse in Connecticut and was cast as Ellie May in a Playhouse production of *Tobacco Road*.

Back in Manhattan that fall, Barbra moved in with a former Erasmus classmate and made do with a series of boring office jobs by day so she could take acting lessons by night.

Miller cast her in Christopher Fry's *A Phoenix Too Frequent,* a one-act comedy, set in ancient Greece. Barbra played the young servant of a rich widow. The new widow, played by Cis Corman, was supposed to commit suicide but was allowed to take a favored servant with her. The play was most notable for starting the lifelong friendship between Barbra and Cis Corman.

Ambitious and hungry to grow, that winter of 1959-1960 Barbra studied with other acting teachers besides Miller: Eli Rill, and the legendary Lee Strasberg.

Others who knew her then recall that she was the only one in her acting class who asked questions, who wasn't passive, wasn't awed by the teacher or the material.

She auditioned for the Actors Studio, but was rejected. Her roommate moved back to Brooklyn and Barbra moved into another tiny fourth-floor walk-up on West 48th Street that she shared with yet another struggling actress. Fired from her office job, she supplemented her unemployment checks by secretly working as an usher at the Lunt-Fontanne Theatre. She always hid her face, so no one would remember she had showed them to their seat.

Playing at the Lunt-Fontanne at the time was the hit musical, *The Sound of Music*. When Barbra heard that "the producers were looking for a replacement for the part of Lisl," she managed to get an audition with Eddie Blum of the Rodgers and Hammerstein casting office. Blum had her sing for three hours, so thrilled was he by her voice, but realistically speaking, there was no place for Barbra in the very Aryan Trapp family or even in the chorus.

After failing to join the Trapp family, Barbra found a new family in the boys in the bars. She went from her failed audition for *The Sound of Music* to a successful tryout at the Lion.

Barbra read the trades like *Show Business* closely, and went on every possible casting call. Her favorite costume for such calls was black stockings and a trench coat: the beatnik look. But nothing helped. They all wanted to know what she had done before.

More showcases followed. There was *Cancer: An American Comedy,* directed by Eli Rill at The Actors Studio, and a production of Karen and Josef Capek's *The Insect Comedy,* which ran for three nights in May 1960 at the Jan Hus Theatre, and in which Barbra got to play several roles including a butterfly and a moth.

And it was in *The Insect Comedy* that Barbra met Barry Dennen, the actor who played a cricket and a snail. Dennen had a popular vocal-comedy act he performed at Village clubs like the Duplex and Showplace. Later he would achieve recognition for roles as Pontius Pilate in *Jesus Christ Superstar* and as the emcee in the London production of *Cabaret.* But in the early 1960's Barry and Barbra were struggling artists.

Barbra and Barry became fast friends, spending a lot of their free time at his apartment in the Village. They shared the same irreverence, intelligence, and love of the arts. He was a world apart from the boys of Flatbush and Erasmus Hall.

Barry and Barbra loved old songs. They would listen to his collection of Fanny Brice records for hours at a time. They were both wild about old musicals, from Shirley Temple to Fred Astaire and Ginger Rogers. They would tape the music off Barry's television and trade the tapes among Barry's friends.

It never occurred to Barry that Barbra herself had a voice until one day she asked to borrow his tape recorder. An agent had asked for a tape of her singing. When Barry heard the first playback he went wild. He immediately told Barbra that she was a born singer, even if she was completely raw and unrefined, almost completely ignorant of the great voices. But Barbra insisted she was not a singer at all. She was an *actress.*

It took a while for Barry to convince her that she should be singing in clubs. She only saw the light when he explained that she would be seen by casting people *and* make money. The Lion, a bar across the street from his apartment on West Ninth Street, had a regular Monday night amateur singing contest. The winner got a week's engagement with free dinners and fifty dollars in cash. He pressed Barbra to enter.

"I agreed to assemble an act for her," Dennen recalls, "if she agreed to physically walk across the street and sign up for the contest at the Lion."

Barry had Barbra study the recordings of Helen Morgan, Ethel Waters, and Mabel Mercer. Gradually, she realized that a song could be acting too, and her feelings about singing changed. But she insists she never imitated these singers. "I couldn't really have imitated anybody," she says, "because I hadn't really *heard* anybody."

Auditions for the Lion's contest were held in the morning. Barbra showed up in jeans, her hair a mess, but the club manager, Burke McHugh recognized the real thing when she started to sing.

That night, Barbra sang "When Sunny Gets Blue" and "A Sleepin' Bee" and emerged the undisputed winner of fifty dollars and a one-week engagement.

From the beginning, word went out that this new artist was a must-see. Agents, trend-setters, club-hoppers. Would-be advisers told Barbra to change her nose and her name. She agreed to a name change only and "Barbara" became Barbra.

It was Burke McHugh himself who took Barbra around the corner for a Sunday night tryout at the Bon Soir, a small but chic cellar club associated with cabaret divas like Mabel Mercer and Sylvia Syms. As Barbra was about to launch into her audition number, "A Sleepin' Bee," she remembered that she still had chewing gum in her mouth. "I took it out and stuck it on the microphone. It got a big howl."

According to Joan Rivers, that wasn't the only thing that got a howl. When Barbra started her audition, Bon Soir owner Phil Pagano shouted from the rear: "Get that broad outta here!" He soon relented and hired her. It was late June, and the club was about to close for the summer, but Barbra was so impressive that they booked her for the first Friday after Labor Day.

That summer, however, Barbra struggled. She was so hard

up she had to give up her apartment on West 48th Street and move back in with her mother in Brooklyn. She landed a tiny part in a summer stock production of *The Boy Friend* in a theater in Fishkill, New York, a two-week run in August. She sang only one song, but fellow actors remember her as exceptional. While others took lunch breaks, she was hard at work practicing her songs.

Back in New York, she spent most of her free time preparing for the Bon Soir engagement with Barry Dennen. The two of them searched for material together. The songs had to allow Barbra to give the kind of dramatic tour de force she loved. Friends like Bob Schulenberg and Terry Leong helped Barbra develop a unique look. Schulenberg, an artist, showed her how to treat her face like a canvas: contouring her cheeks, enlarging her blue eyes by extending her eyeliner and widening them with false eyelashes.

The act Barbra and her friends developed included "Keepin' Out of Mischief Now," "Cry Me a River," and of course, "A Sleepin' Bee."

For her debut, Barbra wore a $4 dress, clown-white makeup, teased hair, pink satin shoes with out-size Minnie Mouse buckles, and "a white-lace-and-pink-ribbon combing jacket, and my mother thought I was singing in my underwear."

The crowd loved her. Headlining comic Larry Storch told her, "Kid, you're gonna be a star."

And Barbra, much as she saw herself as a serious actress, had a genuine rapport with the audience.

"At one time," Dennen recalled for author James Gavin, "she said to me, 'What do I do? They're making a lot of noise.' I said, 'Stare them down. Stand there and think, 'Shut up! Listen to *me!*' One night after she finished up a number, Peter Daniels [house pianist at the club] began the intro to 'Sleepin' Bee,' and Barbra simply stopped singing. Peter kept noodling while she waited for the audience to be quiet. Then you heard a couple of people going, 'Shh! Shh!' The house quieted down and she began the song."

But Barbra was still broke. At the end of her run at the Bon Soir, it was traditional for the performer to give small gifts like cigarette lighters or cuff links to the house musicians. Barbra gave each of the musicians a package of cheese with the supermarket price of ninety-nine cents stamped on the back.

She moved into the Hotel Earle nearby and started looking for an agent. Brief management by a distinguished veteran, Ted Rozar, proved unsatisfactory. Brief representation by another veteran, Irvin Arthur, also proved unsatisfactory, although he had managed to book her on a tour of tiny midwestern clubs.

"Terrified of the audiences, she needed to be almost physically pushed onto the stage, but Barry Dennen had an illustrator friend make a drawing of her looking a little like Audrey Hepburn in *Sabrina,* and somehow that gave her the confidence she needed," recalls Joan Rivers. "Self-conscious about her nose, she considered having it fixed, but Barry talked her out of that. Her act needed polishing, so Barry dragged a recorder to the Bon Soir and between shows they replayed her performance and criticized and improved."

All that work and excitement made Barbra and Barry closer than ever. Soon, they became lovers. He was "her first romantic involvement." But there are differences among Barbraphiles about who ended it and why. One friend told writer James Spada that Barry was insensitive. Joan Rivers seems to believe that Barbra dumped Barry.

According to Joan Rivers, after that first booking at the Bon Soir, Barbra left for the Circus Room in Detroit, asking, "Do you think they have toothpaste in Detroit?" "When she returned from Detroit, Barbra moved out of Barry's apartment," Rivers continues. "Ages later he was waiting for a bus on Central Park West and her chauffeur-driven limousine stopped at the light. Like a Warner Brothers' movie, their eyes met. She mouthed hello and waved her poodle's paw."

Moving on with her career and her life, Barbra left more behind than a beau and mentor. For, until very recently, Barbra has been ambivalent about her large gay following and her roots in the gay community.

"Streisand, whether she likes it or not, became the mother of a post-Garland show-biz phenomenon: the pop diva whose career is launched largely by gay male audiences," wrote Kevin Sessums in a *Vanity Fair* cover story about Barbra. "Following in her footsteps came Bette Midler and now, Madonna."

Bob Schulenberg put it differently: "I have a feeling that Barbra, like Bette Midler later on, felt like a social outlaw, and that's why she identified with them. And Barbra had almost exclusively gay friends in those days."

Yet Barbra claims she was unaware of this connection. "When I won my first talent contest at the Lion," she insists, "I didn't realize it was a gay bar. Cis came opening night after I'd won and I said to her, 'Why are we the only women here?' She laughed and told me where we were."

Why does she think gay men have responded to her throughout her career? "Because I can be imitated," she suggests. "Because I seem bigger than life? I guess because I was so odd."

Three

Meeting Marty Erlichman

"She was the most incredible performer I had ever seen, the wonder of my generation."

—Marty Erlichman

It was during her engagement at the Bon Soir that Barbra first met Marty Erlichman, then a struggling talent agent, operating out of a phone booth with a roll of dimes. He visited her backstage and expressed his interest in representing her. Barbra had already signed with another agent, who, she later claimed, wanted her to change her looks and her name. Erlichman made it clear he would change nothing about her and Barbra would always remember that.

Her initial two-week engagement stretched to eleven as people flocked to the club to see and hear this new talent.

Interviewed in *Architectural Digest* in 1978, Barbra could still recall how she dressed for her opening night: "When I made my debut at the Bon Soir at the age of eighteen, I wore a severe little Victorian blouse with a high black collar. The next day the reviews took as much notice of what I was wearing as they did of my singing. I was a little intimidated, and I didn't want anyone to think I was using my clothes as a gimmick."

If the spring 1961 midwestern tour was Barbra's goodbye to the boys in the bars, it solidified her relationship with the man who would become her manager for most of her career: Martin Erlichman.

When Marty Erlichman had first approached Barbra about representation at the Bon Soir, Barbra probably was already sensing that Ted Rozar was not for her. He had not come up with the big bookings he had promised and their strong personalities often clashed. In Detroit and alone and unhappy, she did not hesitate to call Erlichman in San Francisco and asked him to represent her without compensation. Erlichman agreed and flew to Detroit at his own expense to negotiate a better-paying deal for his client.

A shocked Barbra had learned that she was making merely $150 a night while most singers on the circuit were getting $200 to $250. She wanted Erlichman to get her $200 and meals. He ended up getting her $175 and free dinners and volunteered to kick in $25 of his own money, behind Barbra's back. And he was still not receiving any money from his star.

This was what Barbra needed desperately: the unqualified love and support of a father. Marty Erlichman provided that, becoming, the first and most important of the father figures in her life.

"While in Detroit, Barbra received an invitation to perform on 'The Jack Paar Show.' Up until then, her biggest audience had been the hundred or so people who crammed into the Bon Soir. Ironically, it was through Ted Rozar that Barbra was asked to appear. Guest-hosting the show that week was Orson Bean, Rozar's number one client. It was Wednesday, April 5, 1961. Barbra was given permission to interrupt her engagement at the Caucus Club, and take the first plane ride of her life back to New York City.

Her appearances at the Lion and Bon Soir brought her to the attention of several New York-based shows and she began appearing regularly on Mike Wallace's *PM East* and *The David Susskind Show.* She appeared on *PM East* no fewer than fifteen times in 1961, as a featured singer and resident kook. What she liked best were the talk segments when she got to hold forth on everything from nutrition to Zen Buddhism.

When Barbra completed her tour that April, there were no Broadway offers, so she returned to the Bon Soir, opening for Renee Taylor on May 9. Joe Franklin booked her on a panel with Rudy Vallee several times. And it was while at the Bon Soir that Barbra got her first *New York Times* review: Critic Arthur Gelb wrote that "I went to the Bon Soir to see a comic and was delighted to find such a wonderful new singer on the bill."

Then there were the impromptu, spur-of-the-moment drop-in performances at clubs like the Ninth Circle. But she was unable to break into the better clubs like Upstairs at the Downstairs and the Blue Angel. Desperate for work, she took an engagement in Winnipeg, Canada, that July.

Marty Erlichman understood Barbra's desire to go "legit." He arranged her audition for a new off-Broadway revue, *Another Evening with Harry Stoones.* It was here she originated a whimsical biography in which she claimed she was "Born in Rangoon, Burma, a graduate of the Yeshiva of Brooklyn and Erasmus Hall High School."

On the first day of rehearsals, she vomited. But she impressed the show's creators so much that they added new material especially for her.

Harry Stoones was a ribald, farcical, compendium of sketches and songs and will be best remembered for introducing the talents of Barbra, the late Diana Sands, and Dom De

Luise. Barbra was featured in nine sketches and sang three solos and a duet with Dom DeLuise. She got to play a 1920s flapper, an Indian squaw, and Peter Pan's Wendy. Her song "Value," in which she weighs the advantages of one rich boyfriend against the other, stopped the show on opening night, Saturday, October 21, 1961. Unfortunately, that proved to be closing night as well.

Among those who caught one of the two weeks of previews, however, was her future agent, Sue Mengers. Not that Mengers saw the magic that night. "When I saw her walk out on the stage I thought, 'It sure takes a lot of balls for a *mieskayt* like that to get up in front of people and perform.' It was only after the Morris office got a hold of her and 'fluffed' her, that I saw how beautiful she could be."

Barbra bounced back. That November, she finally made it to the Blue Angel, the smartest cabaret in the city, opening for Pat Harrington, Jr. Located at 152 East 55th Street, the midtown showcase was frequented by show business personalities and producers. Appearing there was a big step, and not just geographically. It took her away from the Village bars with their heavy gay clientele and exposed her to a more middle-class, mainstream audience.

"Streisand was phenomenally successful at the Bon Soir," producer Ben Bagley told James Gavin, an historian of New York's cabaret scene, "but it was very frightening when she went to the Blue Angel, because there was no gay bar there. She had a very conservative audience, a typical Blue Angel crowd, and they loved her."

Among those who discovered her there was Arthur Laurents, who was about to direct a new Broadway musical for David Merrick, *I Can Get it for You Wholesale,* based on Jerome Weidman's best-selling novel of the garment industry. Laurents saw Barbra as perfect for the part of Yetta Tessye Marmelstein, the harried but efficient secretary and he immediately arranged an audition.

MIKE DOUGLAS: "HER TALK AND APPEARANCE QUALIFIED HER FOR A DIPLOMA IN ADVANCED NUTTINESS"

It was also Marty Erlichman who arranged for Barbra's first significant, prolonged, national TV exposure ("that is, when the majority of viewers were awake."), on the Mike Douglas Show. Douglas had seen her act on the late night talk shows and loved what she did with a song. "Her talk and appearance qualified her for a diploma in Advanced Nuttiness," he thought, but he could see that there was something special about her and he wanted her for a co-host.

Marty Erlichman insisted he would not let his future star spend a whole week in Cleveland for the kind of money that Douglas was paying. Douglas insisted he couldn't afford more than scale. He did not want to set a precedent with other guests that could bankrupt his show. Couldn't they work something out? Erlichman suggested: "Find her a gig for a grand in Cleveland."

And they did. They got her a week at a spot called the Chateau in Lakewood for $2,500.

Douglas recalls, "Opening night I wandered over to see how Barbra was doing, and it was less than great. Even for a Monday night the audience was pretty thin. But why not? Nobody knew what a Barbra Streisand was. This was particularly true of a couple of drunks who were heckling her. A few personal remarks were passed, and before you could say Muhammad Ali, Marty was over at their table threatening to punch out the two of them.

"I thought to myself, 'Oh no. I'm not back to this. I'm not ready for this stuff anymore.' Nevertheless, I reluctantly sauntered over to bring my magnificent pugilistic prowess to Marty's defense. Fortunately, before it became my turn, a couple of very large representatives of the management escorted the two troublemakers to the street."

Four

Elliott Gould and Overnight Stardom

"She scared me, but I really dug her. I think I was the first person who ever did."

—Elliott Gould

I Can Get it for You Wholesale was a musical adaptation of a play by Jerome Weidman which had in turn been adapted from his best-selling novel. It tells of Harry Bogen, an unscrupulous, ambitious man who climbs to the top of the garment industry. A sort of New York Sammy Glick. The character of Miss Marmelstein was never key to the story. In fact, according to Weidman, "In our original script, she was, like the desk, just another piece of furniture." But for Barbra Streisand the role of Yetta Tessya Marmelstein was the most important step of her career. A giant step—from singing in small, smoky clubs to holding her own with a cast of theater veterans on the legitimate stage—on Broadway.

Barbra's first audition for *I Can Get it for You Wholesale* was scheduled for the day after Thanksgiving, 1961. She approached it the way she always faced anything that was both important and terrifying: she donned a kooky kind of bravado and proceeded full steam ahead.

For her first audience with the four men who held her fate in their hands: producer David Merrick, director Arthur Laurents, composer Harold Rome, and playwright Jerome Weidman, 19-year-old Barbra showed up in an ancient, honey-colored coat of karakul with fox trim, which she got at a thrift shop for ten dollars.

She started with two comic songs from *Another Evening with Harry Stoones:* "Value" and "I'm in Love with Harold Mengert." When they asked for a ballad, she gave them "A Sleepin' Bee."

Although the four men were impressed, they asked her to come back that afternoon. When Barbra returned to the theater she sang the number sitting in a chair. Why? "One, because I was nervous, and two—because I thought it would be funny to have a secretary moving her chair around the stage with her legs, like a wallflower on wheels." That night, Arthur Laurents came to see her at the Blue Angel. She was hired the next day.

Something else came out of that first audition, however. It was Barbra's first encounter with Elliott Gould.

"I sang," she recalled, "and then I sort of ran around the stage yelling my phone number and saying 'Wow! Will somebody call me, please! Even if I don't get the part, just call!' I had gotten my first phone that day, and I was wild to get calls on it."

She handed out her new phone number to everyone, including the handsome young actor who had already been cast in the lead. His name was Elliott Gould and he came straight from the chorus of *Irma La Douce,* but everyone believed he was destined for greatness.

If Diana Kind had set out to find the perfect husband for her older daughter she might have had someone like Elliott Gould very much in mind. Born Elliott Goldstein, tall, brown-eyed, and Jewish, a Brooklyn boy, he was a prize any mother in Flatbush would have welcomed into her foyer for Friday night supper. And he was on the threshold of a show business career that promised to be every bit as dazzling as Barbra's.

Elliott was impressed with Barbra immediately. "A freak—a fantastic freak," Elliott Gould thought. Later, when he got to know her better, he would say she was a combination of Sophia Loren and Y.A. Tittle.

But that night, after her audition, he did telephone her, but he didn't have much to say. "You said you wanted to get calls, so I called," he said. "You were brilliant."

And then he hung up.

Their paths would not cross again until the first day of rehearsals, when Barbra showed up with a satchel bag and a tattered coat. "She looked like a young Fagin," Elliott recalls.

Barbra was not that impressed with him. "I thought he was funny looking," she later confessed. "He gave me a cigar. He was like a little kid. One day at rehearsals I saw the back of his neck and—I just liked him."

After rehearsals, Barbra and Elliott would walk to the subway together. "She scared me, but I really dug her. I think I was the first person who ever did."

They shared Chinese food and bad horror movies, coffee ice cream and playing pokerino in the penny arcades around Times Square. They became the best of friends. She called him Elly. Later, she would explain: "He did crazy things, I liked him; he wasn't normal." She also admired him as an actor.

Then it happened.

"We were walking around the skating rink at Rockefeller Center when Elly chased me and we had a snow fight. He never held me or anything, but he put snow on my face and kissed me, very lightly. It sounds so *ookhy,* but it was great. Like out of a movie!"

"She was the most innocent thing I'd ever seen," like a

beautiful flower that hadn't blossomed yet. But she was so strange that I was afraid."

But it was not until they were in Philadelphia in tryouts that their love affair really took off. According to Gould, Barbra actively pursued him. On *Wholesale*'s opening night in the City of Brotherly Love, he received a single rose with the message, "From Barbra, to my clandestine lover."

Elliott was a twenty-three-year-old virgin. Barbra was nineteen and only slightly more experienced. The big event happened at the Bellevue Stratford Hotel.

According to Elliott, "Barbra was the one I chose. I was excited, but I was frightened."

But the big moment was nearly ruined when some of his pals suddenly hammered on the door.

"I was trying to become a man and those guys were pounding away," he recalls. "I wouldn't open it. It was my moment and I wasn't about to let anyone take it away from me!"

Elliott and Barbra could not have been better suited. Elliott hailed from the Bensonhurst section of Brooklyn, an only child. Like Barbra, he grew up in a loveless home. "By the time I was three," he has said, "I knew that my parents didn't understand one another, but they stayed together for twenty-seven years."

"My parents should never have married," he told another interviewer. "I remember standing in the darkness of the bathroom when I was three, listening to them bicker, wondering how I could help them get along."

And like Barbra, he shared a desperate drive to become a movie star. As a boy, Gould lived at the movies, growing up on the films of Cooper, Gable, Cagney, and Astair. His mother encouraged him, taking him to lessons and auditions, and up to the Catskills resorts where he won talent contests. Like Barbra, he was willing to do anything to get a role. He told journalists that he got his first Broadway part by ringing the producer of a project called *Rumple* and pretending he was an agent, praising some young kid named Gould. He got the part.

He and Barbra had been raised in cramped, lower-middle-class apartments. Neither ever had a room of their own until they left home: Barbra slept on the living room sofa; Elliott shared a bedroom with his parents.

He and Barbra, poor Jewish kids from unhappy Brooklyn homes, armed with awesome talent and blazing ambition, were about to light up Broadway—together.

Director Arthur Laurents claims that Merrick wanted to fire Barbra almost immediately. "He didn't think she was pretty or funny enough," says Laurents. "On the road, he was right. They just didn't get her. But once we got to New York, everybody got her."

The fact that hers was a minor role or that the producer didn't like her and wanted to fire her, did not discourage nineteen-year-old Barbra from exercising her artistic will.

Out of town with *Wholesale,* Barbra quickly established that she had a director's chair in her future. "I was always a director," Barbra would say when she recalled those early tryouts in Philadelphia. "I had auditioned for the part in a chair, because I was nervous, and I thought it would be interesting staging, and it would be funny. But when I got the part, they proceeded to change the staging—until the night before we opened in Philadelphia, and they said, 'Do it in your goddamn chair,' and it stopped the show. I remember being bawled out the next day, and I couldn't understand why they were so angry at me for being right."

I Can Get it for You Wholesale opened at the Shubert Theatre on Broadway on March 22. Reviews were mixed. But reaction to Barbra was unanimous. She stopped the show. And she had been right about that chair.

Yet her triumph was not without its flaws. She had stolen the show all right—but she had stolen it from the man she was in love with. The show was supposed to make him a star—instead it was Barbra who became the overnight sensation.

"I had very mixed feelings: on the one hand, I loved it; on the other hand, I hated it, because I didn't want Elliott to be hurt."

By the time *Wholesale* arrived in New York, Barbra and Elliott were sharing her $62–a–month apartment. Elliott resisted moving in at first, because the hallway smelled of fish. The railroad flat was over Oscar's Salt of the Sea Restaurant on Third Avenue at 66th Street. Maybe the smell reminded Barbra of her paternal grandfather, the fishmonger.

"The hallway stunk," Barbra admits, "but I didn't care. For the first time in my life, I had my own apartment."

"The only window looked out on a black brick wall," Elliott recalls. "We used to eat on the sewing machine. A big rat named Oscar lived in the kitchen."

The apartment was full of Barbra's thrift shop finds, including empty picture frames. "I had no money to buy art, so I would buy old picture frames and put them on white walls, just framing space, which I thought was beautiful." She had also acquired a dentist's cabinet filled with shoe buckles and an apothecary jar of faded beauty marks.

Elliott grew to love it. "Her taste is just wild, it's genius, really," he said.

Other memories were not quite so happy. There was the bathtub in the kitchen. "One night, we heard a gruesome squealing and scratching," he told Richard Warren Lewis of *Playboy*. "It sounded like a rat the size of an elephant. I looked under the tub and I saw a tail about a yard long with notches on it, probably, to keep score of all the people it had bitten. I closed the door and called the fire department. We used to laugh about that a lot. I look back to Third Avenue with sublime affection."

If Barbra and Elliott were inseparable on stage and off, she

was not as popular with the rest of the cast and crew of
Wholesale. She was cited for lateness thirty-six times and rep-
rimanded by Actors Equity.

Things were especially difficult after the Tony Award nominations were announced and Barbra was the only member of
the company to be nominated. Also nominated in her category,
Best Featured or Supporting Actress in a Musical, were Elizabeth Allen, *The Gay Life;* Phyllis Newman, *Subways are for
Sleeping;* and Barbara Harris, for *From the Second City.*

On April 29, Barbra was in the ballroom of the Waldorf-
Astoria when Phyllis Newman was named the winner.

At least she got a raise, from $150 a week to $200. She
also retained a publicist, Richard Falk, who arranged appearances on "The Joe Franklin Show" and got her name in the
columns. She dropped him after she developed a friendly relationship with one of *Wholesale*'s publicists, Lee Solters,
who would become the dean of show business publicists and
represent her for the next thirty years.

In May, she played a return engagement at the Bon Soir
on May 22, and appeared on *The Garry Moore Show* to sing
"Happy Days are Here Again." The song came about as part
of the show's weekly nostalgia segment, called "That Wonderful Year." For the May 29 episode, they chose 1929, the
year of the stock market crash. One of the songs from that
year was "Happy Days are Here Again," a relentlessly cheerful
number usually associated with events like political conven-
tions. Barbra felt uncomfortable singing it up tempo. So Ken
Welch, the musical director, slowed it down for her. All of a
sudden the lyric took on new meaning, becoming ironic and
dramatic. So Ken and his wife, Mitzi, wrote a verse for it and
created a scene for Barbra in which she is a rich woman who
has just lost all her money in the Crash. Says Barbra: "I've
loved singing it ever since."

Barbra also returned to the Blue Angel as the headliner on

July 16. But by this time she had made a frightening discovery: she didn't much like being on Broadway. She was not the typical Broadway star, not like the legendary Ethel Merman who "froze" her performance opening night and would not change a note or a phrase until she finally left the show maybe years later. Barbra grew restless in the constraints of the show, repeating the same songs the same way night after night. Returning to cabarets allowed her the artistic freedom she craved.

And the Blue Angel was mainstream. Marty Erlichman was working the next career step: a record deal, and it was important to sell Barbra as not just a Village kook nor as merely a comedienne (as she appeared in *Wholesale*). Her future record company had to see that Barbra had the potential to be a superstar.

He and Barbra had set their sets on Columbia, the Tiffany of the industry, but Goddard Lieberson had turned her down. By this time she was being actively courted by Ahmet Ertegun of Atlantic and Alan Livingston of Capitol, but at last, after seeing her at the Blue Angel, and hearing her work on the *Wholesale* and *Pins & Needles* albums, Lieberson called Erlichman: "Look, it takes a big man to admit a mistake and I believe I made a mistake. I would like to record Barbra." She signed her contract October 1. Three nights later, she made her debut on *The Tonight Show Starring Johnny Carson*.

Among those in the subsequent audiences was Frank Rich, a thirteen-year-old boy from Washington, D.C. whose love of theater had influenced him to spend his birthday money to see a Broadway show. He ended up with a ticket to *Wholesale*. "I don't recall why I picked that particular show," he said years later, "maybe it was because there were lots of seats available—but I remember vividly what took place that afternoon at the Shubert Theatre. Most of all I remember a miracle that occurred in the second act. That miracle was Barbra Streisand."

When Barbra materialized on stage, she silenced even the matinee shopping bag rattlers with Miss Marmelstein. "The song uprooted itself entirely from the show that contained it— and for the first time I understood what people meant in movies when they said 'a star is born.'

From then on, Rich was wild about Barbra—"in a wholesome adolescent way of course."

Wholesale closed on December 9. Barbra was relieved. Marty Erlichman had lined up a concert tour to start in March. They had released a single of "Happy Days are Here Again," with a B-side, "When the Sun Comes Out" the previous November, but with little support from Columbia, and a mere 500 copies shipped, it sank like a stone.

Barbra recorded another single, "My Coloring Book," with "Lover, Come Back to Me," on the B side, again without attracting much attention.

Despite the lackluster performance of her first two singles, Barbra and Marty Erlichman were convinced that she still had a brilliant recording career ahead of her. Since she had first attracted attention in clubs, they intended to launch her with a live album. That November Columbia Records set an engineering crew up at the Bon Soir and recorded Barbra's performances, among them "Keepin' out of Mischief," "I Hate Music," "Nobody's Heart (Belongs to Me)," "Cry Me a River," "Who's Afraid of the Big Bad Wolf?" "I Had Myself a True Love," and "Lover, Come Back to Me."

But *Barbra Streisand at the Bon Soir* never happened. Barbra retained creative control and even this early in her career did not hesitate to use it. Unhappy with the results, she vetoed the entire album.

On January 23, 1963, Barbra went into the Columbia studios and recorded eleven songs in three days for what would become

The Barbra Streisand Album, a collection of the songs she had performed at the Lion, the Bon Soir, and the Blue Angel.

Already she was insisting on perfection and control of all aspects. She'd approved a photo for the cover but when she saw the cover something seemed off. It was her nose! Some well-meaning soul at the lab had retouched her photo, removing the slight bump on her nose. Barbra told the lab people: "If I wanted my nose fixed, I would have gone to a doctor." Later, when she listened to the record before release, she noticed something odd: weird dead spaces between the phrases. She asked about it and was told "We cleaned it up, took out the breathing." She said: "Don't *clean* so good. You're cleaning up what is natural, what is right."

Barbra was now getting between $2,500 and $7,500 a week for concerts. It began with a triumphant return to the Blue Angel that January. In spite of a New York City newspaper strike, she was hailed in the national press.

The tour was arranged by Marty Erlichman, working with Joe Glaser, president of Associated Booking. Barbra's first agent, Irvin Arthur, had left Associated Booking to handle Bob Dylan, and Barbra had been taken over by Glaser.

Barbra plugged the upcoming tour with appearances on *The Tonight Show Starring Johnny Carson,* March 5.

Johnny Carson and Barbra had a special relationship. She had appeared on *The Tonight Show* on October 4, just two nights after he had taken over the show. He was a genuine fan and continued to have her back on the show once a month for five months, until her March 5 appearance on the eve of her 1963 concert tour to support *The Barbra Streisand Album.*

Barbra's concert tour officially started in Miami in March at the Cafe Pompeii of the Eden Roc Hotel. She shared billing with Sergio Franchi.

Elliott Gould was soon to leave for London to rehearse for the West End revival of *On The Town.* The producers and

Elliott himself had wanted Barbra to join him in the light-hearted musical, but Marty Erlichman talked her out of it. He did not think she should leave the country at such an important time in her career. The show opened in London on May 26 and was not a success.

But Barbra was triumphing from coast to coast. She followed her so-so engagement in Miami with three weeks at the Hungry i in San Francisco, which had much more in common with the sophisticated clubs she had played in New York.

In April she went to Mr. Kelly's in Chicago and spent a week cohosting the *Mike Douglas Show* in Cleveland, while she played the Chateau there.

By the time she returned to New York that May, *The Barbra Streisand Album* was showing up on *Billboard*'s top-forty albums chart. Its top spot was number eight, but the album held on for seventy-eight weeks.

She also spent a week in Los Angeles to prepare for her appearance on *The Dinah Shore Show* May 12, and she cried every day. It was her first separation from Elliott.

She played Basin Street East in New York that May 13, sharing the bill with Benny Goodman. The club was at 48th Street and Lexington Avenue, but the lines outside to see Barbra stretched to Third Avenue, a block away.

That same month, Barbra was invited to sing in the White House for President John F. Kennedy. Merv Griffin was the host of the annual White House correspondents' dinner that May 23, 1963. The entertainers who had been lined up included Edie Adams, comedian Marty Brill, and Barbra. Recalling the evening in his autobiography, Griffin confessed: "I now have to make the *painful* admission that we'd turned down Barbra as a guest on *The Merv Griffin Show;* and I was still doubtful that she was right for this dinner."

Merv knew that JFK liked beautiful starlets, a category that hardly fit Barbra. But Barbra stopped the show that night.

"Washington's power structure sat mesmerized as the little girl from Brooklyn stunned them right out of their minds," he recalled. "When she finished, an awesome pause filled the room; then applause thundered toward the stage. Everyone in the room—even me—knew they were looking at a girl on her way to becoming a major star."

And most of all, she made an impression on the President. "Mr. Kennedy was jovial after the show and had kind words for all of us," said Griffin. "When I introduced him to Barbra, she curtsied, then stuck a program and pen in his face and said, "May I have your autograph?"

"I wanted it."

"Well, I know, but they specifically asked us not to stop the President."

"But I wanted his autograph, Merv. How many times would I get a chance to have the President sign an autograph?"

"Well, did he write an inscription?"

"Yes. 'Fuck you. The President.' "

Not only did Barbra get the President's *real* autograph, but the picture of her getting it made all the morning papers, said Griffin.

That June Barbra began recording *The Second Barbra Streisand Album,* again on a tight schedule. While awaiting its September release, she embarked on her historic summer 1963 tour which included the Coconut Grove in Los Angeles, Harrah's at Lake Tahoe, the Hollywood Bowl, and the Riviera in Las Vegas, and a sold-out one-woman concert at Chicago's 5,000-seat Arie Crown Theatre.

Liberace had wanted to work with Barbra since he first saw her at the Bon Soir, but his managers felt Barbra lacked the glamour of his usual partners. He and Barbra had been booked for the same Ed Sullivan Show and during rehearsal everyone in the theater stopped what they were doing to listen to Barbra sing. Finally, after hearing Barbra sing at Basin Street East, he insisted on bringing her to Las Vegas.

At first Barbra wasn't sure she wanted to sing for gamblers, but Liberace's offer of $7,500 a week convinced her. Unfortunately, opening night, August 4, threatened to be a fiasco.

Barbra's brash Brooklyn manner and eccentric looks and style mystified the middle-American audience at the Riviera. She drew barely polite applause at the first show. After an equally disastrous second show, Liberace revamped the show, "introducing" Barbra as his discovery, thus giving her his endorsement.

On the strength of this, the audience warmed up to Barbra and the Riviera bosses stopped talking about firing her. But it was too late to stop the *Hollywood Reporter* review that observed: "Her makeup made her look like something that just climbed off a broom, but when she sang, it was like the wailing of a banshee bouncing up and down on marionette strings. It wasn't until she does three or four songs that her voice is noticed as being very pleasant. Her outrageous grooming almost nullifies her talent."

According to Liberace's biographer, Bob Thomas, the showman had to urge his Riviera bosses to sign Barbra, telling them that she would be "a big, big star." They resisted until Liberace presented a third show, something casinos sometimes stage on Saturday nights so that other performers can see the new acts in town. Before an audience of her peers, Barbra was electrifying. The Riviera signed her to a long-term contract at $20,000 a week.

During Barbra's run at the Riviera, producer Ray Stark and composer Jule Styne flew in to see her perform. They were considering her for a role in a musical comedy they were working on based on the life of Stark's late mother-in-law, the Ziegfeld comedian Fanny Brice.

Stark was immediately impressed. "Barbra was unique," he

said. "She had the aura and charisma of Fanny Brice on stage as well as that incomparable voice." In her hotel suite, Styne, the composer behind such classic Broadway musical comedies as *Gypsy* and *Hello, Dolly!*, played songs he had written for the show about Fanny Brice, which Stark intended to produce. After two weeks at the Riviera, on August 21, Barbra opened at the Coconut Grove in Los Angeles to a cheering crowd of celebrities. That night Ray Stark made an agreement for her to star in *Funny Girl*.

Among those in the audience at the Coconut Grove: Actress Lesley Ann Warren and her husband Jon Peters, owner at the time, of a chain of hair salons. "When Barbra sang, whatever it was, the power she had—the magic in her fingers and face—controlled the entire room," he later recalled.

Among the Hollywoodites who wooed Barbra during her three-week run were the agents Freddie Fields and David Begelman, who even put a Rolls Royce at her beck and call. When her contract expired with Associated, she signed with their agency, CMA. In her free time, Barbra started working on the *Funny Girl* score with Styne and his lyricist, Bob Merrill.

By the close of her engagement at the Coconut Grove, Elliott had returned from London where he had closed in *Our Town* and they were reunited. He accompanied her to her stint at Harrah's in Lake Tahoe.

When Bill Harrah saw her perform in rehearsal, he had the same reaction as Phil Pagano at the Bon Soir a few years earlier: "My God, I can't have her in my show!" he is said to have screamed. "She'll scare the customers out of the room." Liberace assured him Barbra would be well received, particularly when he introduced her as his discovery.

Liberace never failed to take credit for giving Barbra one of her first important breaks. According to Bob Thomas, many years later, as the star lay dying, his last moments were cheered by listening to Barbra's just-released *Broadway* album.

Actually, there was a serious reason why Elliott had flown to Barbra's side in Vegas. He had heard rumors that she was having affairs and he was determined to confront her.

According to Gould, Barbra told him: "I can't really stay with you. It's not comfortable. I have to sow my oats. What if I was with you, and I wanted to be with Marlon Brando?"

But Gould refused to give up. He continued to woo her.

They had reached a turning point in their relationship and they both knew it. They could either marry and make a life together, or they could go their separate ways.

"It was like we shook on it," Elliott recalls. "Let's get married—glop! So we did." He and Barbra drove to Carson City and were married there on September 13, 1963. By then, *The Second Barbra Streisand Album* was moving quickly into Billboard's Top Ten. Barbra's two Martys, Marty Erlichman, her personal manager, and Marty Bregman, her business manager, were their witnesses. Harrah's provided a big house for the honeymooners, and Barbra turned domestic and announced she was giving a birthday party for the stage manager. What's more, she was going to bake the birthday cake herself.

It turned out to be individual cakes for all the party guests. Barbra watched expectantly as they blew out the candles and started to eat. "Do you like it?" she asked.

"Well," Liberace said slowly, "the frosting is a bit tough."

"Oh," said Barbra, "I ran out of sugar so I used flour instead."

On October 6, Barbra appeared on the new Judy Garland show, doing a duet with Judy, she singing "Happy Days" juxtaposed with Judy's "Get Happy." She also joined Judy and Ethel Merman to belt "There's No Business Like Show Business." Barbra was so good she won an Emmy nomination for "Outstanding Performance in a Variety or Musical Program," the first time in Emmy history that a guest appearance had won such a nomination.

The following night, Barbra performed at the Hollywood Bowl, on a bill with Sammy Davis, Jr.

After Barbra returned to New York late in 1963 it was announced that she had copped the plum of the 1964 Broadway season, the role of Fanny Brice in *Funny Girl.*

Back in New York, Barbra and Elliott gave up the Third Avenue apartment and moved into a new place appropriate to a star. They found it at 320 Central Park West, a grand duplex on the twenty-sixth and twenty-seventh floors.

For Barbra 1963 had been a banner year. She had been named Best Female Vocalist of 1963 and *Cue's* Entertainer of the Year. She showed up on the covers of *Life, Look, Time, Show,* and *Cosmopolitan.* Suddenly, people were talking about a Streisand look, a Streisand style, a Streisand sound.

The close of the year found Barbra philosophical about her success so far: "Some people look at me and say success has gone to my head, but that's not true," she complained that October 1963. "I've always been this way. I'm no good at dealing with people, at being tactful. I say whatever is on my mind. I go by instinct; I don't worry about experience. I mean, if there had been only one war, then you could listen to people who say they know all about things, but experience hasn't counted for very much, has it? People feel something and they argue, and sooner or later it builds up and pow! you hit somebody."

But even as Barbra was marrying her Prince Charming she had begun a business relationship with another father figure: the producer Ray Stark. Their love-hate business affairs would outlast her romantic marriage and bring both Barbra and Stark some of the greatest achievements of their respective careers.

Five

Barbra the Broadway Baby

"When we were finally in rehearsals for Broadway—now, this was before the girl was a star, she was just this strange little, creature who walked out at her first audition looking like a russian Cossack—she had her manager write me a note telling me that there were two songs she didn't like, 'People' and 'Don't Rain on My Parade.' She didn't think she wanted to sing them. I called her right up and said, 'Barbra, if you don't sing "People," you don't sing my score.' "

—Jule Styne

Ray Stark was looking to cast a romanticized version of the life story of his mother-in-law, the legendary Fanny Brice, a vaudevillian, actress/singer/comedienne. Stark, a Hollywood producer and former agent for Marilyn Monroe and Richard Burton, had made a name for himself with a number of commercial films, most notably *The World of Susie Wong*, starring William Holden and France Nuyen.

Funny Girl originated as a biography culled from notes the great Ziegfeld Follies star Fanny Brice had dictated shortly before her death in 1951. Her son-in-law, movie producer Ray

Stark, reportedly paid $50,000 to have the book plates destroyed when he decided to turn the Brice story into a screenplay. Finally, it became a play by Isobel Lennart, which Stark planned to produce as his first Broadway venture.

Stark had originally intended to cast someone like Anne Bancroft or Carol Burnett, until a friend of his wife, Fran, saw Barbra in *Wholesale* and told them how much Barbra reminded her of Fanny. He resisted the idea at first, believing that Barbra was too young for the part.

After seven grueling auditions, and with the backing of Jule Styne, Barbra was cast. "After we cast her," Styne recalls, "I even flew to Las Vegas where she had already been booked as the opening act for Liberace, and taught her the score between shows—that is, when I could drag her away from the gambling tables."

THE BEGELMAN CONNECTION

Back in 1961, when he was trying to sell *Funny Girl* as a film script, Stark had wanted Judy Garland to play the title role. He had to approach her through her agent, David Begelman, who had just started Creative Management Associates with his partner, Freddie Fields. Judy Garland was their most important client. She was not interested.

Three years later, when Stark decided he wanted Streisand for the Broadway musical, he found himself again dealing with David Begelman, who in the meantime had added Barbra to CMA's roster of clients. Because of a loophole in Stark's original contract with Barbra, Begelman managed to obtain a substantial increase in her salary for the Broadway run of *Funny Girl,* costing Stark more than half a million dollars beyond what he would have had to pay under the original deal. Although Stark was livid, he and Begelman became good friends. Each recognized that the other was a skilled street fighter, with qualities they mutually admired.

FUNNY GIRL

Barbra joined the *Funny Girl* company as it headed for out-of-town tryouts in Boston late that December. Gossip around Broadway already had it that the show would never make it to New York. Boston was bad, and the next stop, Philadelphia, was even worse. No one questioned Barbra's talent, but she seemed skittish and insecure and sometimes ignored the audience. Those in the balcony complained she was not projecting.

Script doctors were called in, and director Garson Kanin was replaced, possibly at Barbra's request, by Jerome Robbins. Sydney Chaplin's role as Nicky Arnstein was whittled away, in spite of rumors of a relationship with Barbra.

Clearly, the untested young star was not hesitating to assert herself. Jule Styne still marvels at the *chutzpah* of the young Streisand: "When we were finally in rehearsals for Broadway—now, this was before the girl was a star, she was just this strange little creature who walked out at her first audition looking like a Russian Cossack—she had her manager write me a note telling me that there were two songs she didn't like, 'People' and 'Don't Rain on My Parade.' She didn't think she wanted to sing them. I called her right up and said, 'Barbra, if you don't sing 'People,' you don't sing my score.' "

Barbra had yet to establish that she could carry a show. But she loved the whole rehearsal process. The out-of-town tryouts, the endless rewrites that Broadway veterans found so grueling, just thrilled her. She considered it all great fun!

"I would eat these huge Chinese meals right before I would go on stage," she reminisced. "The more they changed the scenes, the more I liked it. The more I had different songs to try out, the more I loved it. We had 41 different last scenes, the last one being frozen only on opening night. Forty-one versions of a last scene! That was always exciting, stimulating."

Jule Styne concurs: "There is only one way to deal with Barbra Streisand," he would say years later. "If you don't tell her the truth, then you're going to have problems."

"You've got to be straight with her," says Styne. "This reputation about being difficult comes from untalented people misunderstanding truly talented ones. Because she's so talented she had a tendency—maybe she still does—to show off a bit. She was always shoving shovelsful of her talent in your face. Jerry Robbins summed her up. He said she does everything wrong, but it comes out right."

Finally, after five postponements, four changes of directors, endless reorchestrations and forty rewrites of the show's last scene, *Funny Girl* finally opened at the Winter Garden Theatre on March 26, 1964 at a then-record cost of $750,000 and made theatre history. "Everyone knew Barbra Streisand would be a star," wrote Walter Kerr, "and so she is."

"Some stars merely brighten up a marquee: Barbra Streisand sets an entire theater ablaze," raved a *Time* critic.

Soon Barbra was on the covers of *Time, Life, Show,* and *Cosmopolitan*. She appeared in *Vogue* three times in 1964. Some dubbed her "kooky" but Eugenia Sheppard, doyenne of the fashion editors, insisted: "She's about as kooky as Gloria Guiness, C Z Guest, the Duchess of Windsor, or any of the all-time fashion greats when they had just turned twenty-two."

But it wasn't all fabulous. "Opening night was a disaster for Barbra," Elliott revealed later. "People were pawing her, sticking mikes down her bosom, telling her things she couldn't believe.

"It was almost depressing.

"I had to realize that Barbra is *my* woman, but everybody

wants her. I have to be above it, because if I'm in it I'm going to get stomped to death."

FUNNY GIRL NOT SO FUNNY BACKSTAGE

Barbra was not popular with the rest of the cast and company backstage. There was the incident with ambitious understudy Lainie Kazan, who had the nerve to call the press when she went on for the ailing star. The coverage was nothing like the raves for Barbra, but enough to see that the next understudy who was hired, Linda Gerard, had a clause in her contract that if she ever did go on for Barbra she would not notify the press. If she did, she would be fired.

GLAMOUR

Overnight, Barbra was a star. The girl who "wore wool and dreamed of fur," was photographed lolling seductively on leopard, skunk, seal, and silver fox pillows in a story for *Life* magazine that revealed that she had "ten fur outfits and eight hats, and not one of them is all-purpose."

To no one's surprise, Barbra was nominated for a Tony Award as Best Actress in a Musical.

She still had trouble getting the respect that was due her. Columbia, which had the first option on the original cast recording for *Funny Girl,* passed it up incredibly, and it was released by Capitol Records. Meanwhile, sales on *The Third Barbra Streisand Album,* released on February 10, 1964, were somewhat disappointing.

Barbra finally had her first hit single in "People" which was released early in 1964 and hit the *Billboard* top-forty singles chart on May 23, 1964. Her next album, *People,* released that September, became her first *Billboard* number one hit.

One week in 1964 Barbra had five albums listed among

Billboard's 100 best-selling albums in the country, including *People* in first place.

And every night she played to SRO crowds at the Winter Garden. Celebrities like Audrey Hepburn, Elizabeth Taylor and Richard Burton, Lauren Bacall, and Jason Robards visited her backstage.

Barbra was even getting mail from Frank Sinatra, who wrote after seeing her in *Funny Girl:* "You were magnificent, I love you."

But she was still shy around her fans, ill at ease at the celebrity parties she and Elliott were supposed to attend for the good of her career and the show.

Barbra resented criticism that claimed she was not giving her all, that she didn't have the stamina and discipline of an Ethel Merman or Carol Channing. "It was never true that I had no discipline," she told journalist Pete Hamill. "It's just that I *never* played to the balcony. I always played to the best seat in the theater. I always played to my own reality."

Elliott was the one person she could completely trust, could be completely honest with. "Barbra is basically a very simple girl," he said years later, "and I'm really as simple as she is. One of our conjugal delights actually *was* eating Nathan's hot dogs—whether we did it in the back seat of a [chauffeur driven] Bentley, or at the mother church in Coney Island."

The old boredom and restlessness that set in during *Wholesale* returned. Barbra focused on her apartment, her marriage, her Italian lessons, piano lessons, publicity, and interviews. She even showed up at the Grammy Awards on May 12 that year. She had been nominated in three categories: "Happy Days are Here Again," for Record of the Year (she lost to Henry Mancini's "The Days of Wine and Roses"); best vocal performance by a woman; and the big prize, Best Album of the Year for *The Barbra Streisand Album.*

She was up for an Emmy for her appearance on *The Judy*

Garland Show, but lost to Danny Kaye of *The Danny Kaye Show.* The biggest disappointment, however, was the Tonys. *Funny Girl* had eight nominations, including for Best Musical and Best Actress in a Musical. She lost out to Carol Channing for *Hello, Dolly!*

That June 22, it was announced that Barbra had signed with CBS for a series of television specials. She was to receive $5,000,000 for ten years at a special a year. She would have complete creative control.

She also made time to prepare and rehearse for her outdoor concert at the Forest Hills Tennis Stadium. On July 12, 1964, in spite of a driving wind and threat of rain, she performed before 15,000 people.

The awful truth was that the show had stopped being fun for her the minute it opened. "Once they froze the show, I felt like I was locked up in prison. I couldn't *stand* it anymore. I could hardly even get through the performances." The whole experience made her begin psychoanalysis "twenty-two years too late."

Barbra was already developing deep conflicts about the very act of performing. As *Funny Girl* dragged on, "I was scared. Performing made me nervous, sick. I was scared I wouldn't connect. Really, I prefer TV or movies to the theater. I'm afraid of audiences now."

Her boredom with the routine of eight performances a week showed on stage. Frank Rich, the boy from Washington who had fallen in love with her at thirteen when he saw her in *Wholesale,* had remained a devoted fan. He bought her first three albums and played them over and over again. Her television specials had become important events in his life. When Barbra got her first starring role on Broadway he worked feverishly to contrive circumstances that might force his parents to send him to New York to see it. In the meantime, he listened to the original cast album until he knew the show's song lyrics by heart.

When he finally got to the Winter Garden, he watched with mixed feelings. "I saw that Fanny Brice was the perfect role for Streisand in her new incarnation as full-fledged star," he said later. Fanny Brice was, after all, a Miss Marmelstein who made good. "But the actual experience of seeing *Funny Girl* was the first major disillusionment in my unrequited love affair with Streisand." To young Rich, "Her performance suggested that she had a certain amount of distaste for the customers who had paid to see her."

"Clearly bored with her long run in the show, Miss Streisand mugged like crazy, she fooled around with the melodies and lyrics of her songs, recited her lines without conviction and ignored her fellow actors." Rich claimed Barbra treated her leading man, Sydney Chaplin, "as a hired hand who was on stage merely to feed her cues. It was not a pleasant afternoon in the theater."

Although Barbra was on top of the world, headlining a Broadway show, the start of the year 1965 found her contemplative.

"YOU CAN'T ASK SOMEONE HOW TO BECOME A STAR"

"People should never ask other people for advice," she told an interviewer. "You must feel things yourself and know innately what to do. If it's not your own thought, it can't solve your problem. You can't ask someone how to become a star.

"Reality can never live up to a dream. I can't remember what I expected in specific terms, except of course that I never thought of any of the bad things that come with success. *C'est la vie.*"

"I was fortunate not to have to work in cheap nightclubs

or in the chorus. I could never be in the chorus. I admire people who can, but it's not right for my temperament."

Barbra was invited to appear at Lyndon Johnson's Inaugural Eve celebration on January 18. But a botched lighting cue rattled her and spoiled her performance.

Barbra had other problems with LBJ. "I sang for Kennedy because I loved him—it was so incredible. He actually *glowed*. But when I sang at Johnson's inauguration, it was the most depressing evening I ever had. Kennedy was dead and it was just awful."

That January she also launched into a punishing schedule: playing eight performances of *Funny Girl*, while rehearsing for her television special on her non-matinee days.

"MY NAME IS BARBRA"

Barbra's first television special *My Name is Barbra*, her first and last special in black and white, aired on the CBS Network on April 28, and established her versatility and her new high-fashion image. The variety special featured solely Barbra, surrounded by stylish sets, lavish props, and fabulous production numbers.

One memorable nine-minute segment was a fantasy set at Bergdorf Goodman. She sang and flitted about the street floor of the Fifth Avenue specialty shop in opulent furs including a $15,000 full-length Somali leopard coat for her grand entrance, white mink knickers to play a newsgirl, a long evening suit of white broadtail mink and a velvet jump suit with a matching robe lined in the finest Canadian wild mink. The TV audience watched her stomp on the mink.

"I used to hate mink," Barbra said during a fitting for the show, "But now I appreciate it for its solidity."

The eccentric from Greenwich Village was suddenly right at home in Bergdorf's. "I really didn't like boa scarves as much as they said I did," she assured fashion reporter Marilyn Bender, "I like simple elegance, neat. I'd rather change my jewelry and have a few things and wear them all the time. A person is more important than clothes. A dress should fade out of sight but greatly."

That September 12, *My Name is Barbra* swept the Emmy Awards. Barbra took time out from *Funny Girl* to join the ceremony at the New York Hilton (also simultaneously broadcast from the Hollywood Palladium on NBC). Breathless, giddy and apologetic for a run in her stocking, she accepted her Outstanding Individual Achievement Award in Entertainment and told the crowd: "This is too fantastic. When I was a kid—I mean a younger kid—my favorite shows were the Oscars and Emmys. I didn't care who won then, just how they looked. Television is a marvelous business. This is my first experience with it. I figured out that I would have to work 58 years in *Funny Girl* to reach as many people as I did in one show." *My Name is Barbra* also garnered Emmys for Outstanding Program Achievements in Entertainment, for Outstanding Individual Achievement Awards for her director Dwight Hemion, Tom John, her art director, Bill Harp, her set decorator and Peter Matz, music director, and Joe Layton, for conception, choreography and staging.

A VISIT FROM LIBERACE
(OR BARBRA GETS BORED)

Barbra was bored by the routine of nightly performances. When Liberace turned up in a matinee audience, she interpolated "I'll Be Seeing You" into one of her musical numbers for his amusement. He and his associate were invited backstage and Barbra greeted him with affection: "Gee, you must really like this show—you've been here four times!" she said.

Lee studied her stylish orange dressing gown and said, "I'm glad to see that you're dressing with some class, Barbra."

"Oh, this," she said. "I wore it in the show but they cut the scene, so they let me keep it.

Later that night Barbra turned up at Liberace's show at the Royal Box of the Americana Hotel in a blonde wig.

LOUIS KIND DROPS IN

There were other surprise visitors backstage at the Winter Garden. Even Louis Kind showed up. One day, Barbra scratched the cornea of her eye and her understudy was preparing to go on in her place. "Everyone was telling me not to go on because I might hurt my eye," she told Ryan O'Neal. "Then I got this card and a little dish of candy from my stepfather—he was out in front, in the audience." Barbra insisted on going on. Doctors anesthetized her eye so it wouldn't tear and she went on. "I never did a show like that," she said. "It was the best performance I ever gave." After the show, Barbra went backstage and waited for her stepfather, but he never came back.

"She never saw him again," O'Neal recalled. "but she kept the candy container. That's why I like Barbra—because all of those things in her life have enriched that woman."

"WE LIVE DAY-TO-DAY"

But the stress of her success was already beginning to take its toll on the Hansel and Gretel marriage of Elliott and Barbra. "We live day-to-day," Barbra told Shana Alexander. Elliott added: "To say I love Barbra—that's obvious. Otherwise, I couldn't have stood it. I know the traps, I know the wounds, and I've decided it's worth it to wage the battle. People say theatrical marriages don't work. Our battle is especially difficult because we're real people, not just two profiles, two beautiful magazine covers. We really love one another."

As she settled into a long run, Barbra turned her attention to making a home. She hired interior designer Charles Murray, and together they worked.

"Look, this was my first real home," Barbra recalled years later. "Let me tell you, I wanted Louis, Louis, Louis—as much as I could lay my hands on. And I got it: bronzes, porcelains, satin, moire. Later I became far more sophisticated."

She and Elliott had settled into their duplex penthouse with its terraces, living like gypsies with a kitchen crammed with TV dinners and Breyers coffee ice cream. And a 300-year-old carved bed mounted on a dais with a refrigerator beside it, draped and curtained in olive-gold damask and a red fur bedspread. The bed was the first serious antique they bought together.

"There's been no intermediate stage in my life," she wailed. "I went direct from a railroad flat to a duplex penthouse."

STRESS WITH ELLIOTT

Unfortunately, as Barbra's career blossomed, Elliott's seemed to wane and he was cast into the shadows. Together they formed two production companies, Barbell and Ellbar Productions to develop projects. But no one was interested in projects that did not come with Barbra attached.

There were hints of stress in her marriage. "Everything affects your marriage," she admitted. "You have to give up certain things, make compromises if you both have careers. But some husbands don't like their wives to work in an office either. When two people are mature, it doesn't matter what their professions are."

FEUDING WITH RAY STARK

Everything had seemed so bright when Barbra, still heady with overnight stardom, had signed her contract with Ray Stark in 1965. The agreement called for Barbra to make multiple pictures for his company, Rastar. She had only wanted to commit to one, namely *Funny Girl,* but shrewd businessman Stark refused to make the deal unless she signed a four-picture deal. She was not willing to risk losing *Funny Girl.* But she had come to regret the pact.

That December 17, Mike Frankovich, Columbia Pictures's vice president in charge of production, announced that the studio had signed to make the film version of *Funny Girl.*

After nearly two years, Barbra left *Funny Girl* on December 25, in order to recreate the role on stage in London. When the curtain came down, she was overwhelmed by the intensity of her emotions; she broke down on stage and was completely unprepared for the cast and audience singing "Auld Lang Syne" back to her. That last performance was the only time she ever sang "My Man" at the Winter Garden. "I did it for Ray, because he loved it," she said later. "And I did it for Fanny Brice. After all was said and done, it was still her song."

Six

Barbra Goes to London
and Makes a Baby

"As an artist, it wouldn't be right for her. All she'd make is money."

> —Marty Erlichman explains why he and Barbra turned down an invitation to play Shea Stadium.

Late in January 1966 Barbra journeyed to the Philadelphia Art Museum to film her second network special, *Color Me Barbra,* her first in color. Another sequence took place at a circus created for the event. "Chaos threatened again," Barbra recalls, "the lights were hell on the penguins, a lion broke out of its cage, and a baby elephant roared so loud that a nearby llama nearly suffered a heart attack."

With *Color Me Barbra* completed, she was ready for a vacation. She had just been named one of the Ten Best-Dressed Women in America, and that March she would be on the cover of *Vogue.* Already planning her third special, Barbra intended to wear high fashion couture. The first week of February she flew to Paris to review the spring collections with a company that included Elliott, Lee Solters, and Marty Erlichman, and a reporter and photographer from *Life* magazine.

In the following week, Barbra saw the shows at the houses of Chanel, Gres, Yves Saint Laurent, Dior, and Cardin. She also had an audience with Coco Chanel.

Ray Stark gave a dinner party for her at Maxim's.

Barbra chose nine costumes from The House of Dior for her next special and after a series of fittings she vowed "Never again. They rush you too much," Barbra complained. "The only clothes I liked were from Dior. All that cut-out stuff is not for me."

Barbra and Elliott were off to spend a marvelous three-and-a-half weeks touring Europe—Paris, Rome, Marseilles, Nice, and Florence.

In keeping with Barbra's new high-fashion image, she was photographed by Richard Avedon for Vogue. The photos and the accompanying interview by Polly Devlin ran in the March 15 issue. "Capture me correctly," the twenty-three-year-old star warned the photographer. She modelled Dior and Madame Gres, her hair by Alexandre.

Devlin described the scene at Avedon's studio, as he rushed in with a record player blasting out Barbra's own voice and said: "That's my favorite record, just listen to that *note,* it's the greatest, isn't it?"

"I've never thought about it," Barbra replied. Avedon played it again and she listened, saying, "I sure held it a long time. You know, I used to have a fight with the instrumentalist about who would end first. I said we should end together." They ended together.

Later, the story takes on a poignant tone as Barbra muses about her success: "At eighteen I dreamed of success and it was much easier because dreams were clear. When you reach success it's no longer exciting. You have to learn and you learn it's never as good as the dreams. It's sort of anti-climactic,

you know? I don't think I'll ever have enough confidence.
I'm never satisfied with anything I do. I never think it good
enough."

FUNNY GIRL GOES TO LONDON

That March Barbra reluctantly reprised her role in *Funny
Girl* in London. Ray Stark had insisted, telling Barbra that
if she wanted to do the film she had to do London. He
apparently believed that the exposure was critical to creating
a foreign audience for the film.

Barbra arrived in the city on March 20, accompanied by
her dresser, her secretary, Marty Erlichman and his wife, as
well as a four-man BBC crew preparing a *Barbra Streisand
Arrives* special. Elliott had come ahead to find them a place
to live and after a brief stint at the Savoy they settled into
a flat in Ennismore Gardens.

The production was directed by Lawrence Kasha, with Michael Craig as Nicky Arnstein, and Kay Medford and Lee
Allen reprising their roles from the Broadway production.
The theater was the 2000-seat Prince of Wales. Right from
the start, it was an ordeal for Barbra. She confided to her
leading man, Michael Craig: "Two and a half years ago
when I started the show in Philadelphia it was such fun and
everything was marvelous. Now it's all so difficult and I
don't get any fun out of it any more." In spite of rumors
about conflict with her understudy and missed performances
and shortened choruses, Craig assured friends that Barbra
was a total professional. "I have no complaints about Barbra," he insisted. "She is a star in the real sense of the
word and I have nothing but admiration for her."

Following the opening on April 13, 1966, the show drew

mixed reviews, but Barbra was lauded, taking six curtain calls.

During the London run, another fabulous beauty visited Barbra backstage at the Prince of Wales Theatre. Sophia Loren dropped in the very night Barbra returned after three days battling gastric flu.

Elliott had wanted to audition for the Nicky Arnstein role on Broadway, but never got a reading. This time he was offered the role in London, but he turned it down.

MARTY ERLICHMAN

Marty Erlichman's plan was to proceed cautiously with Barbra's career. "The main thing," he told one interviewer, "is to guard her against too much public exposure as a performer. She demands a lot from an audience and people can only take so much of it at a time."

By that time Erlichman was fielding 600 requests for concerts—some offering as much as $50,000 a night. He refused to let Barbra play such locales as New York's Shea Stadium or the Houston Astrodome: "As an artist, it wouldn't be right for her. All she'd make is money."

COLOR ME BARBRA

Color Me Barbra aired on March 30 on CBS and got excellent ratings and reviews. It included Barbra performing leaps and flips on a trampoline. She put herself through risky training sessions for a few seconds of high flying comedy. She swung on a trapeze, bounced on a trampoline and tap-danced through sawdust.

She hated the trampoline, complaining that it gave her a

feeling of limbo, "absolutely limbo, so you don't know where you're at."

In the circus sequence, Barbra, clad in silver sequins and orange-leather boots, played ringmaster to a pony, elephant, leopard, llama, tiger, anteater, baboon, and a squad of penguins and pigs.

BARBRA'S PHILOSOPHY

By now Barbra was recognized as an international star. She sensed resentment among some of her old friends and associates, but she dismissed their claims that she had changed. "I want to do things the way I feel, and I don't care if other people disagree with me. But I didn't just get that way because I got a part in a Broadway show. I was like that when I was twelve years old. I've always said what I thought and acted the way I thought was right for me.

"Mostly I don't like actors; they're only concerned with what's going on inside of them all the time, preoccupied with their own emotions. I don't care for singers, either, they're all bound up with the way they look, with what's going on outside of them. I guess I've got enough going on inside of me to keep me busy.

"Nobody really knows me, who I am. I don't even know myself. I hate talking about myself. I hear it and I hate it. I've always been a mixture of self-confidence and insecurity. I want to be something and make something. I don't care what. Acting and singing aren't enough. You can't put your hands on them, they're too ephemeral. I want to make something I can touch. I bought a Singer sewing machine; I want to be able to do something with that.

"And I want to be famous. I don't care whether it's by

singing or acting or what. I want everybody to know my name, even the cowboys."

NESTING

The duplex apartment now boasted five antique chandeliers, including one in the bathroom, but the finest was in the dining room. Deep red patent leather lined the kitchen walls. A collection of antique hats and shoes was stored in the sewing room. A great Aubusson rug dominated the living room.

The small but opulent foyer was lined by red damask wallpaper and Barbra's seven gold-record albums and other awards, and a framed letter of thanks from President Johnson for her appearance at his inaugural ball, and an eighteenth-century French desk.

The foyer led to a small den which had a Steinway and a paisley love seat. Barbra liked the fabric so much, she had a dress made to match.

Barbra was miserable during the pregnancy. According to a proposal for his as yet unpublished autobiography, Gould claims that when she was seven and a half months pregnant she locked herself in the bathroom sobbing: "I don't want your child."

BARBRA'S MILLION DOLLAR BABY

One week before *Funny Girl* opened in London, Alan King, the comedian, and his business partner, Walter A. Hyman, announced that they were sponsoring a planned five-week, twenty city tour of the United States for Barbra later that year, for which Barbra would be paid $1 million—more, even, than Sinatra. But the tour was not to be. On April 18, she announced that she was pregnant and all tour plans were canceled, including the Chemstrand special. The press dubbed Barbra's unborn child her "million dollar baby."

"This pregnancy is like a God-given thing," Barbra gushed, "and the timing couldn't have been better. I was beginning to feel like a slave to a schedule. Pretty soon I'll have nothing to do but cook and be pregnant five whole months. I can't wait!"

"Why do they say that?" she said. "I mean, why must they measure everything in money? The most important thing is not what got canceled but that a healthy baby is born.

"I always thought that having babies was for other people," she said, "but not for me." She revealed that she used to dream about having a child, but didn't believe it was possible. She had even thought about adopting one.

"I can't suddenly get poor for her or him, can I? But I don't want a child who has nothing but toys from F.A.O. Schwarz. Kids like simple things to play with: a piece of paper, a walnut shell. They should be dirty and basic when they want to be. I don't want to make her a kid brought up by the book. I think that if I can give her confidence and love and the feeling that she's wanted I'll be able to be honest, too; a person as well as a parent. That's the important thing; that she feels loved and has *both* parents."

With her typical thoroughness, Barbra had begun to read medical books. She had always been fascinated by the way bodies work and she was not squeamish about the sight of blood. She gushed to one reporter: "Each organ has a duty in the process, each part of it set off by complex signals. . . . I'm telling you, it's not to be believed. There *must* be a God!"

She was thoroughly committed to the idea of natural childbirth. She and Elliott planned to take classes together when they returned to New York.

"I can't understand how some women can just say, 'Give me an injection, I don't want to know a thing about it.' I mean, I really wonder about people like that."

She immediately cut back on her schedule in *Funny Girl,* and on July 16, 1966 she gave her final performance. Without Barbra, the London show closed immediately. She flew back to New York the next day and continued to work, showing up for a Columbia sales convention at the Sahara Hotel in Las Vegas to promote *Color Me Barbra,* the soundtrack recording of her television special.

July 30, a visibly pregnant Barbra sang at the Newport Music Festival in Rhode Island, and broke the attendance record set by Frank Sinatra. She played more concert dates in Atlanta, Philadelphia, and Chicago that summer, before retiring to Sands Point on Long Island Sound. In August, a pregnant and pensive Barbra posed with a group of British schoolboys for a fashion feature in Ladies Home Journal. That September, she returned to work on her next album, *Je M'appelle Barbra.*

On December 19, at 3:00 P.M., Jason Emanuel Gould, seven pounds, twelve ounces, made his arrival at Mount Sinai Hospital in New York.

"I ALWAYS KNEW I WOULD BE FAMOUS"

"I always knew I would be famous," she boasted. "I knew it, I wanted it. I always wanted to be out of what I was in. Out of Brooklyn. I had to get out. I was never contented. I was always trying to be something I wasn't. I wanted to prove to the world that they shouldn't make fun of me. The girls sometimes made fun of me. When I got to Manhattan, where people really *live,* I couldn't train myself to keep one hand in my lap. Now, I love formal dining and place cards.

"But it doesn't make me feel comfortable. I'm not comfortable sitting down to a formal dinner. I'm more comfortable standing up and eating out of three pots on a stove. I love Cokes and cones and French fries, that taste of bacon, like you get in greasy spoons. I love greasy spoons. My mother and I, we never went out to eat. She didn't pay much attention to me.

"Recently, after a late party, I was all dressed in diamonds and furs, and I had this urge for rice pudding without raisins. Some people like it with raisins, I like it without raisins. Well, I had this urge and every place was closed, but Elliott found a waterfront diner that was open. . . . We could have gone to the Automat, I suppose, I like the Automat. You put in the nickels and get what you want—pies, cakes, sandwiches. But you know, nowadays, it's hard for me to go to the Automat. I mean, people *know* me and inhibit my eating."

SUCCESS

Success hardly seemed to have changed her. She had a passion for cold cucumber soup, but she had also discovered the chocolate souffle at "21." She still liked to wander into Chinatown restaurants and try out her Chinese by ordering items that were not on the menu.

Her one indulgence, a second-hand, cream-colored Bentley ("Less obvious than a new Rolls"), exploded in a cloud of smoke in Central Park that February, and she now drove a Chrysler.

"Basically, I find her more responsible," said one close friend. "She is altogether nicer, more thoughtful, more concerned about everything. Yet she seems calmer, too."

She settled into her apartment as well. Her seven gold records lined the hallway leading to the tiny den where a Steinway piano held some original Fanny Brice sheet music. Also on display: signed photographs of Presidents Kennedy and Johnson.

But there was a price: a loss of privacy. "Kids stand downstairs with cameras and ask if they can ride downtown with me," she said. "And, like, I'm eating in a restaurant, spare

ribs or something, and they stand there waiting for an autograph while you get a napkin and dry your fingers. Sometimes
they come up and ask for it for their daughter, and I say, 'Oh,
you don't like me, right?' "

PERFECTIONISM

Her drive for perfection was stronger than ever. It was well
known that she might rerecord an entire song because she
thought one note was off. She involved herself in everything:
costumes, sound, production design. "I have fifty ways to do
everything," she told one interviewer. "I love it when a director makes up my mind for me. I wish they would do it more
often. I don't know why they don't. Maybe they're afraid."

FUTURE PLANS

She insisted that she had no plans further than that January.
"Why should I?" she asked. "I'd like to do movies, maybe.
I'd never do a TV series. Well, maybe later, but now—ugh!—
no. It's worse than doing a Broadway show. I don't like to
work that much. We taped for forty hours for the eight-minute
sequence in the museum. Maybe if I only did TV shows, or
only records, it would be fun."

"I'd like to do the least I can to be remembered."

She opened at the Prince of Wales Theater on April 13, 1966.
The London Drama Critics voted Barbra the Best Foreign Actress and *Funny Girl* the Best Foreign Musical of 1966.

Two months after the opening, Barbra and Elliott announced
the impending birth of their first child, making front page news
on two continents. On December 29, 1966, Jason Emanuel was
born.

The child was conceived, partly, Elliott later acknowledged,
because "we had heard having a baby could be a solidifying

thing for a marriage." Barbra took natural childbirth lessons and Elliott would give her breathing exercises every day. But she had a difficult delivery, a breech birth, and Barbra was in the intensive-care unit for a whole day.

Barbra was probably relieved to see the show close. Years later, she would confide to interviewer Gene Siskel that those last months in the show had been the origin of her notorious stage fright. During those last few months on stage, "My mind used to go blank. And that frightened me—that absolute lack of control." The London production of *Funny Girl* proved to be the last time Barbra appeared on a legitimate stage in a performing capacity.

It was in 1966 that Barbra released her first bilingual album, *Je M'appelle Barbra,* in which she sang in both French and English. It included her first songwriting effort, called, appropriately enough, "Ma Premiere Chanson," which translates as "My First Song."

Seven

Barbra Hits Hollywood
and Meets Omar Sharif

"The first impression is that she's not very pretty. But
after three days, I am honest, I found her physically beautiful, and I start *lusting* after this woman!"

—Omar Sharif

Barbra began 1967 reveling in her new role: mother. Jason
Emmanuel Gould was the most important man in her life after
Elliott. Significantly, she turned her sewing room into a nurs-
ery. But Jason's little bassinet and crib had pride of place in
Barbra's gold and white dressing room. And little Jason him-
self was a perfect angel.

"He's great about sleeping in the morning," she told an
interviewer. "I give him a bottle at ten at night and he doesn't
wake up until seven tomorrow morning."

Elliott was busy rehearsing the starring role in a new play
by Jules Feiffer, *Little Murders*. It would take him out of town
to Boston and Philadelphia for tryouts, and by the time the
play opened on Broadway Barbra would be scheduled to go
to Los Angeles to start filming *Funny Girl*, the movie.

Barbra did find time to film her third CBS network special,

The Belle of 14th Street. Original plans for a high-style, high fashion concept special with couture clothes from Dior had been scrapped in favor of a nostalgic look back at turn of the century vaudeville. Barbra was paired with Jason Robards, Jr., who could hold his own in their scenes from *The Tempest* but who was no song and dance man.

The second half of the special featured Barbra singing music hall standards like "I'm Always Chasing Rainbows," "Mother Machree," and "My Buddy" solo and was much more effective. The show would air on October 11, 1967 to mixed reviews.

Meanwhile, Ray Stark had been attending to getting the movie version of *Funny Girl* made. In spite of studio objections, he insisted that Barbra star in the role she had created on Broadway. The story of Fanny Brice had actually inspired two earlier films: *Broadway through a Keyhole* (1933) with Constance Cummings and *Rose of Washington Square* (1939) with Alice Faye and Tyrone Power. But this would be the ultimate film version of her story.

"TO ME, BEING A STAR IS BEING A MOVIE STAR"

The continued business relationship between Barbra and Ray Stark had become a true marriage of convenience. Each of them needed the other.

Stark did not want to film *Funny Girl* without Barbra in the title role and Barbra did not want him to film it without her. Bringing the Fanny Brice story to the screen had been Ray Stark's dream for more than twenty-five years and he was not going to blow it now. But his public statements and Barbra's gave little hint of the bitter behind-the-scenes wrangling.

Barbra was widely believed to be collecting one million dollars for her movie debut, but, according to Stark, she was getting only $200,000. He refused to give her a percentage of the box office gross. The rumored million dollars included subsidiary rights such as soundtrack royalties.

That May, a month after taping *The Belle of 14th Street,* Barbra arrived with baby Jason in her arms, accompanied by Elliott and her poodle, Sadie. She was excited and thrilled to be beginning this new stage of her performing career. She told reporters gathered at a press conference: "To me being a star is being a movie star."

Barbra arrived in California on May 2, already contracted to do three films for three different studios: *Funny Girl* for Columbia, *Hello, Dolly!* for Fox, and *On a Clear Day You Can See Forever* for Paramount.

"I don't feel they were taking a chance on me," she said. "You see, we're only ourselves. We have only ourselves to sell. And everything I'd ever done, I'd done on my own—it made money for someone else."

In spite of the contracts, Barbra still had to submit to a screen test which Herb Ross directed. He and Barbra were both pleased with the results: her unique charm transferred to celluloid.

"This is just like going to the movies, isn't it?" she remarked during the filming. She seemed totally at ease in front of the cameras. Her confidence was reinforced by veteran cinematographer Harry Stradling. "Those tests were beautiful," he reported to *Photoplay* magazine. "Garbo was special, Dietrich was special. No great star conformed to the norm. And Barbra is in that classic tradition." As for her nose, Stradling was emphatic: "I *like* the nose," he said. "No, you can't make Barbra look like Marilyn Monroe. But she *does* have a beautiful face—because she's got something back of it."

Barbra later praised Stradling: "Anybody who is really a pro and talented appreciates other talent, it's only the mediocre who are threatened." More significantly, she requested him for all her subsequent films, until his death in 1970.

Barbra and Herb Ross also grew close. "I was there holding

her hand the first day she saw herself on screen," Ross recalls. "I couldn't believe how she could be so unerring in angling her face to the most flattering light. I discovered her secret: she has incredibly sensitive skin and is guided by the warmth of the light on her face."

As Ross noted, however, Barbra was "extremely lucky" to have had two years to work on her first movie role.

Funny Girl, the movie, had originally been scheduled to begin production that January with Sidney Lumet directing, but it had been postponed because of Barbra's pregnancy. At last, Stark settled on the legendary William Wyler, who had already accumulated thirteen Academy Award nominations and three Oscars. He had worked with some of the most difficult women in the movies and he was the great love of Bette Davis's life. He had not, however, ever directed a musical before, and so Herb Ross was named to direct the musical sequences.

Wyler was quite taken with Barbra: "She's no great beauty," he acknowledged, "but the appeal comes from way inside and makes her damned attractive," he said.

Barbra arrived on May 2. Six days later Richard Zanuck of 20th Century Fox announced publicly that she would star in the film version of *Hello Dolly!,* playing the eponymous widow of a certain age, the role created on Broadway by Carol Channing. First the $10 million dollar production of *Funny Girl,* now *Dolly;* no wonder veterans in the business regarded the newcomer warily. No sooner had she arrived than Barbra began to alienate Hollywood veterans and the press. Her outspoken nature and her naivete combined to make her vulnerable to an establishment that seemingly had it in for her from the beginning.

Barbra tried to make sense of their attitude and recognized that some of it sprang from jealousy and some of it came from a feeling that she hadn't paid her dues, she hadn't "earned" her enormous success. "I came out with the role all ready," she acknowledged. "I wasn't the underdog."

And then there was the matter of her appearance. "In terms of Hollywood standards, where everything is so perfect—hair, nose, everything—well, I came out here without doing any of those things like having my nose fixed or teeth capped or changing my name."

In an effort to launch Barbra in Hollywood and introduce her to the Hollywood community, Stark and his wife Fran threw a party for her on May 14 at their Bel Air estate. It was a disaster. She and Elliott arrived ninety minutes late. Barbra clung to her husband and barely spoke to John Wayne, Cary Grant, Rosalind Russell, Natalie Wood, or any of the other 300 guests. When presented to Marlon Brando, the man she had watched for hours on the screen at Loew's, all she could say was: "What are you doing here?"

Soon Barbra and Elliott took refuge in the Starks' library. "I didn't know any pictures would be taken," she said. "This will give you an idea of what you're in for," she was told.

Barbra was still new to the ways of Hollywood when she arrived for what she thought was to be a private dinner with Rock Hudson, only to find press and photographers camped outside his house. She made a polite appearance and quickly departed.

"Revolting . . . all those photographers . . . I didn't know people invited photographers to parties in their own homes," she complained.

Barbra was more nervous about Hollywood than she let on. "I'll have a problem in Hollywood with the hours," she confided to Sheila Graham. "I don't get up before 12:30 in the afternoon and I can't leave the house before 2."

Heady with success, naive about the press, Barbra sometimes came across as arrogant. "Sure, the money's rolling in," she told one journalist. "What am I supposed to do—shout 'Stop?' "

Marty Erlichman could now boast: "Barbra is a $100 million business." He computed her earnings at $3 to 4 million a year and estimated she would be around for 30 years.

The men who ran Hollywood had never seen anything like her. Certainly, they had never seen this kind of attitude from a woman.

Ray Stark treated Barbra like a star—she not only had her own chair, her poodle Sadie got one too—but he resisted letting her see the day's rushes.

When Barbra finally did step in front of the cameras, it was not in Hollywood, however, but in New Jersey. Her film career actually began in Jersey City on July 11 as she stepped from a train onto a railroad station platform. Early scenes were shot there and in New York. Barbra quickly tired of the endless retakes that are part of the filmmaking process. After spending more than an hour to film a single one-minute scene, Barbra became vocal. "They give me a chair with my name on it. So when do I get to use it?" she complained. It was the middle of July, she was dressed for the winter of 1915, and had to make the same thirty-yard dash down Pier 84, trying to catch up with Nicky Arnstein's departing ocean liner.

Ray Stark reminded her that the scene was costing tens of thousands of dollars. Barbra pretended to be horrified. "Oh, my God, I can't act on anything so expensive, Ray," she said. "I gotta talk to you!"

Once again, as with the cast and crew of *Funny Girl*, the Broadway musical, Barbra alienated her colleagues. Model Carolyn Kenmore, who played one of the ten Follies Girls, complained that Barbra kept cast and crew waiting in the heat while she ate. She was also watchful about perceived threats. "The word was out that Miss Streisand had looked over the Ziegfeld Follies Girls and anybody she considered too pretty was getting reshuffled to the back row. I had never seen a woman so bold, so uncouth, so unfeminine in my entire life."

Recalling her own experience, veteran actress Anne Francis complained in the *Hollywood Reporter* that her role had been cut from "three very good scenes and a lot of other ones, to two minutes of voice-over in a New Jersey railroad station." She tried, unsuccessfully, to have her name removed from the credits.

"Barbra ran the whole show—Ray Stark, Willie Wyler, Herb Ross," Francis said. "She had the Ziegfeld Girls scenes changed—one day she told Wyler to move a girl standing next to her because she was too pretty, and the girl wound up in the background. . . . It was like an experience out of *Gaslight*. There was an unreality about it."

"I just got off a Julie Andrews picture," one tired dancer told John Hallowell of *Life* magazine. "Julie was just one of us, one of the kids. Nice, professional, but not my idea of a movie star. But Streisand! The moment she walks on—like it's the way Joan Crawford must have walked on!" He looked down at his feet, "I think I hate her."

Musical conductor Walter Scharf described her sound as "one part jazz, one part humor, one part pure drama and ten parts soul," but when asked to work on two later Barbra Streisand musicals, he declined, saying "Once was enough."

OMAR SHARIF

One man who was not intimidated by Barbra was her co-star, Omar Sharif. The darkly handsome Egyptian with the limpid brown eyes first attracted attention in *Lawrence of Arabia* in 1962, followed by *Dr. Zhivago* in 1965. He had been cast in the role of Nicky Arnstein after Marlon Brando and Gregory Peck had turned down the role and Ray Stark had vetoed Frank Sinatra. As Sharif himself put it, "The screenplay was built around Barbra. What actor would agree to play her straight man?"

From a set next door where he was finishing a western, Omar often wandered over to watch Barbra work. "The first impression," he acknowledged, "is that she's not very pretty. But after three days, I am honest, I found her physically beautiful, and I start *lusting* after this woman!"

"If all the Jews and Arabs got on like Barbra and Sharif, there would never be a war," said William Wyler.

Sharif began filming his scenes with Barbra that September, a few days after the Arabs and Israelis were locked in the Six-Day War. The investors, producers, and most of the key people on the film, including the star, were all Jewish and all painfully conscious of the fact that her co-star was an Egyptian.

As Sharif remembers it, Barbra's own mother declared: "My daughter isn't going to work with any Egyptian!" Ray Stark discussed breaking his contract. Fortunately, Wyler settled it: "If Omar doesn't make the film I don't make it either!" He also stated: "Arabs and Jews have gotten along for centuries, until twenty years ago, anyway. Why not in my picture?" That was enough for Barbra, who added: "We people of the theater don't think of ourselves by race or creed. We have our own standards of judging each other—and that's talent.

"The biggest reason for that outbreak among my people and his was hatred. Nothing real has been solved by rage and bitterness. My feelings toward Omar are ones of affection and admiration, and I'm sure he feels the same toward me."

That subdued protests for a time, but the cinematic teaming of the Jewish Streisand and the Arab Sharif made international news again when photographs of their on-screen kiss were widely circulated and Sharif was censured in Cairo. Sharif responded: "I don't make it a point of asking a girl her nationality, her occupation, or her religion before kissing her— either on-screen or off."

By then, Sharif acknowledged, he had fallen under Barbra's spell.

The unpleasant beginning gave way to a happier story. As Sharif recalled in his memoir, *The Eternal Male,* "While *Funny Girl* makes me remember an unfortunate political situation, it's also connected to a wonderful love story."

Because he and Barbra fell in love.

Romance blossomed between these two opposites from two different, even hostile cultures. Sharif already counted Sophia Loren, Julie Christie, and Anouk Aimee as conquests. Now, "Barbra Streisand, who struck me as being ugly at first, gradually cast her spell over me. I fell madly in love with her talent and her personality."

As Sharif recalled in his autobiography, "Barbra's villa served as our trysting place. At the time, my own villa housed my family. We spent our evenings, our weekends at her place." There they led the simple life of people in love. They had no need to go anywhere else. They would cook. Sharif would prepare his Italian specialties; Barbra would heat TV dinners.

Still in spite of their efforts to stay private, they were spotted at a fashion show, and another time necking in a Los Angeles restaurant. The rumors reached Elliott in New York. Barbra dismissed them as just that: simply rumors.

On November 30, Columnist Sheila Graham reported that the Barbra Streisand-Elliott Gould union was "a trifle shaky" and that Elliott had telephoned Barbra from New York where he was filming *The Night They Raided Minsky's* to berate her for being seen with Omar.

Graham reported that talk of possible trouble between Barbra and Elliott had begun when Omar escorted Barbra to an exclusive fashion show at the Factory disco. Then they were seen dining at a fashionable restaurant.

"I'm furious with Barbra and told her that," said Elliott. "She should have known that she is in a very difficult position out there, where the press doesn't like her because she has been uncooperative.

"I'm a very secure person but as a man I have certain reactions. But I can tell you I am furious with my wife for putting herself in this kind of position."

"Why in hell did you go to the fashion show with Omar?" he demanded. "Because the ticket would have cost me $250," she replied.

Ever-faithful, Elliott told Graham: "I'm much happier in my career than she is in hers. I'd rather she was a housewife than a great big star, but she has this enormous talent." Barbra, he insisted, was "terribly naive," and "just a little girl from Brooklyn."

Although Barbra has acknowledged that she loved Sharif, she remains coy about how far the mutual admiration went. She would usually deflect questions about the relationship with a simple response: "He's a very unique person."

Later, she would complain: "I don't like lies told about me, and the press, when I first got to Hollywood, created all sorts of tales. They had Omar and me in bed every night of the week. If we had done that, *Funny Girl* would never have been made."

On another occasion: "It got so I couldn't wait to get on the set in the morning. The day I knew I was going to work with Omar were happy days. The days he didn't have to work were miserable. I know Omar knew I was 'ga-ga' over him but he was too much of a gentleman to make a play for a married woman. I would read in the columns where he took this girl and that girl out. It used to make me feel actually sick. I fell hopelessly—madly—in love with my leading man. It sounds like the old Hollywood story—a B-movie script—but it actually happened. And I don't care who knows it. I loved every second of it."

Sharif could also be changeable on the subject of Barbra. In one television interview he claimed he still had feelings for Barbra. "Something lingers on," he said. "With Barbra Streisand in *Funny Girl*, it was different because I was in love with her, I really was and it was one-sided, yet I did love her a lot. She had a lot of affection for me, but it just didn't go beyond that."

And here is Sharif in another interview: "I am sorry to become involved in the breakup of any home, especially when there is a baby involved. But people do fall in love no matter what the circumstances and, sadly, no matter what the consequences."

In his memoirs, Sharif said that the two most remarkable women he ever met in his life were Anouk Aimee and Barbra Streisand. He later blamed his translators for anything in his memoirs that might have offended Barbra. "The choice of words in some cases are not choices I personally would have made," he said.

He also complained to Rex Reed that Barbra upstaged him. "She's a monster. I had nothing to do but stand around. But she's a fascinating monster. I think her biggest problem is that she wants to be a woman and she wants to be beautiful and she is neither."

"BARBRA IS GOOD. WITH WILLIE WYLER SHE'S GREAT."

Pete Hamill, who visited the set, reported watching Barbra go through take after take of some scenes. Occasionally, Ross would finish, say the scene was fine, please print it, and want to move on, and then Barbra would have an idea, some minor alteration, and they would go through it again and she would be *right* and the scene would be marvelous.

At other times, Hamill observed, she was just moving a simple scene into more baroque version. Producer Ray Stark would look in once in a while, knowing the production was behind schedule, hoping it would catch up. No, he told Hamill, there had never been any question that anyone but Barbra would play the lead in the movie.

"Barbra is good," Stark told Hamill. "With Willie Wyler, she's great. When she was a success in the play, there was no question about who would do the movie. I just felt she was too much a part of Fanny, and Fanny was too much a part of Barbra to have it go to someone else. Sure, there's always an element of risk when you take someone who has never made a film and put her in a $10,000,000 production. But this is *Barbra Streisand!* Plus Willie Wyler. Plus Herb Ross."

Wyler, a small, white-haired man who smoked long filter-tip cigarettes, told Hamill: "Barbra can do anything. We haven't asked her to do anything that she can't do. And she does it half a dozen different ways and that makes my job easier. She's not the most relaxed person, but neither am I. She worries about everything. I think that's fine. Lots of people don't worry about anything, but I'd rather have her worry too much than too little."

Barbra resented the rumors that she challenged Wyler's authority or tried to take control from him. "I have opinions and ideas and Willie respects them and I respect him," she said. "I don't know why people make a big deal out of it. I don't know what other actors do. Do they just sort of stand around there like mummies, get dressed, get told what to do, move here, move there? Do they do that? That can be pretty boring for the actress and director, besides what it does or does not do for the performance. . . . Of course I would always do what he wanted to do. He's the director."

A few years later, Barbra elaborated on her feelings in an interview with Wyler's biographer, Axel Madsen: "At the beginning, I guess, before we started the picture, we had the usual differences most people have. At that point I think I knew more about *Funny Girl* than Mr. Wyler. I had played it a thousand times and had read all the scripts—for the movie and the play. But once we started . . . well, it couldn't have been a more creative relationship. I don't know what people are used to. . . . We tried different things and experimented and so forth. It was stimulating and fun and good things came out. And, I guess, bad things, too. But, I mean, it's the only way to work."

Barbra felt that she and Wyler understood each other instinctively. He would go: "Oomph, a little more oomph," and Barbra would say: "Okay, I know what you mean," and give it a little more oomph. She was the first actress he allowed to view rushes with him. "He knows I'm not destructive," Barbra said. "I'm very objective about my work."

Wyler defended his star: "She's not easy, but she's difficult in the best sense of the word—the same way I'm difficult."

A HAPPENING IN CENTRAL PARK

Barbra began musical rehearsals for *Funny Girl* on May 4, 1967. She took time off from filming to fly to New York for an outdoor concert in Central Park on June 17. After less than two days to rehearse, and under the constant threat of rain, Barbra sang before an estimated crowd of 135,000 fans who had gathered to hear her in the Sheep Meadow. Barbra's free concert in Central Park would yield a television special, *A Happening in Central Park*, and another record album under the same title.

A few weeks later, on July 9, Barbra gave a sell-out concert for 20,000 in the Hollywood Bowl.

When Barbra gave these two outdoor concerts she was the perfect professional on-stage. Few were aware of her private terror and the terrible strain she was under when she performed live.

Years after the *Happening in Central Park*, Barbra told film critic Gene Siskel that the concert marked the beginning of her notorious stage fright.

"There were 135,000 people there. My movie [*Funny Girl*] was going to be banned in Egypt. The government had said that [because Omar Sharif] was an Arab and I was a Jew, they weren't going to play any of my movies. So I was afraid that somebody might take a shot at me during the concert. So I started walking around the stage fast. And I forgot my words, which is an actor's nightmare." It was the same thing that had happened to her during the last months of *Funny Girl* on stage. The complete loss of control terrified her.

"I could never imagine wanting to sing in public again," she said.

That summer, Elliott had few offers, but one would mark a turning point for him. Appearing in *Luv*, a comedy with Shelley Winters in Nyack, New York, he was seen by director William Friedkin who put him into *The Night They Raided Minsky's*. (The deal was negotiated through Barbra's agent, David Begelman.)

At the same time, Barbra was closely involved in preproduction plans for *Hello, Dolly!*, involving numerous long telephone discussions with producer Ernest Lehman.

Many felt the role should have gone to Carol Channing, but producer/writer Ernest Lehman disagreed, believing that Channing's personality would not translate to the big screen.

"I did feel that *Dolly* was a story of older people and they should hire Elizabeth Taylor to play her," Barbra told an interviewer. "I thought that would be a great role for her first musical. But when everybody seemed to be against me as Dolly [except producer Ernest Lehman and 20th Century-Fox], I took up the challenge. I've never been an underdog in Hollywood, and people get spiteful about me. They tell lies that make good journalistic copy. I have very little in common with a character like Dolly, who fixes people up and lives

other people's lives. I do share the fun she gets in bargaining
and buys, and can understand her experience as a woman who
has loved and lost. A woman can be any age for that. But I
really didn't respond to the Broadway show—a piece of fluff.
It's not the kind of thing I'm interested in."

What Barbra was interested in was real life, real people,
and playing Medea. "*Dolly* takes place in an age before people
realized they hated their mothers—the whole Freudian thing,"
she explained. "So it wasn't something I could delve psycho-
logically into too deeply, but I could have fun with Dolly and
get days off because I didn't have to be in every single scene
for once. I call *Hello, Dolly!* my last big voice picture."

Barbra praised the music: "I think Dolly's whole score has
been underrated. It's much more than just a one-song show."

December 1, principal photography on *Funny Girl* was
completed. At the wrap party, she gave Wyler an antique gold
watch engraved "To make up for lost time." Wyler gave her
a director's megaphone and a musical conductor's baton. Ray
Stark gave her a ten-minute short on the making of *Funny
Girl*. The end credits acknowledged "Produced and Directed
by Barbra Streisand." It was his idea of a joke.

After the picture wrapped, Sharif considered the affair
wrapped as well, leaving Barbra desolate. Years later, he would
try to explain the end of the four month fling in his autobiography: "The years have gone by and I say to myself that
Fanny Brice loved the hero of the movie, that she didn't love
Omar Sharif; that I loved the heroine . . . that I didn't love
Barbra Streisand."

It was just the way he was, he explained. "They say I'm
pathologically unfaithful. No. I'm never unfaithful. I simply
fall in love a lot, often and fast."

Barbra returned to New York for the holidays and to be
with Elliott, who was wrapping *The Night They Raided Minsky's*. Around that time, she first saw the short story "Yentl,

the Yeshiva Boy," by Isaac Bashevis Singer. She instantly recognized that it would make the kind of movie that she wanted to make.

Barbra returned to standards for her next album, *Simply Streisand,* which was released this year. Later in 1967 she would release *A Christmas Album* of holiday favorites.

FEUDING AGAIN WITH RAY

In November, while Barbra was still filming *Funny Girl,* Stark submitted two proposed musicals to her: *Wait Till the Sun Shines Nellie* and *Two for the Seesaw.* Her contract gave her ten days to consider them before responding to Rastar. Barbra responded that she would only consider them if she was given script and director approval, but soon rejected both properties anyway. She had no interest in doing another musical immediately.

Stark was not like her Village chums and was not to be so easily dismissed. He filed suit on December 28, in Superior Court in Los Angeles. Meanwhile, her contract with him for the film version of *Funny Girl* gave him exclusive use of her services from May 4, 1967 until completion of production.

Somehow nobody mentioned this clause when Barbra gave her concerts at Central Park and the Hollywood Bowl. The Central Park happening, of course, had also become a TV show and sound track album. Now Stark's suit sought not only to block the airing and release of the special and the album, it also demanded he receive all the proceeds she received from the concerts and anything related to them.

It took months before Barbra's lawyers and Stark's lawyers managed a compromise and Stark dropped his suit.

Barbra could keep her money and she would fulfill the four picture contract with Stark. But she would not have to do *Wait Till the Sun Shines, Nellie* or *Two for the Seesaw.* She would do the film version of the 1965 play, *The Owl and the Pussy-cat*. It was just a detail in their ongoing love-hate relationship. Neither held a grudge. When the cast and crew of *Funny Girl* gave Stark a surprise party, Barbra was there to sing a parody of "My Man": "Oh Ray/I love him so/If some footage I can't see/I say, 'Oh Gee/So What?' "

Stark always publicly defended his star: "The only thing she hasn't learned is tact."

Eight

Feuding with Ray Stark
and Walter Matthau

"The only thing she hasn't learned is tact."

—Ray Stark

"She steps on your head and your tail. She's gotta wave her goddarn feathers across your balls and in your eyes, otherwise she's not happy."

—Walter Matthau

The last days of 1967 were marred by an open rift with Barbra's main mentor and father figure, Ray Stark. On December 28, his company, Rastar, had filed suit in Los Angeles Superior Court, charging Barbra with breech of contract. On January 17 he sought an injunction to prevent Barbra from working for any other employer, contending that she could not work for anyone else during filming of *Funny Girl* or work in any other film without Rastar's consent.

It would be months before Barbra's lawyers and Stark's lawyers managed a compromise and Stark would drop his suit. Barbra would ultimately keep her money and she would have to fulfill the four picture commitment to Stark. But she would not have to do *Wait Till the Sun Shines, Nellie* or *Two for the Seesaw.* Instead, her next picture after *On a Clear Day You Can See Forever* would be the film version of a 1965 play, *The Owl and the Pussycat.*

On a happier note that January, Elliott joined Barbra and other Hollywood celebrities and stage personalities who attended a "Broadway for Peace" performance at Avery Fisher Hall at Lincoln Center in New York.

And she purchased the film rights to "Yentl, the Yeshiva Boy." She could not have known at the time that it would take her years to make the picture, or that it would be such a monumental success. All she knew was that the story gripped her from the moment she read the first words: "After her father's death . . ." Barbra felt an immediate connection to the material and knew she had to turn it into a film.

Later that month, she and Elliott flew to Europe for a brief vacation. She was back in California by February 13 to report for wardrobe fittings and to discuss costume sketches with Irene Sharif for *Hello, Dolly!*

Throughout her career, as intensely as she has immersed herself in a project, Barbra has always simultaneously looked to the future. So, in typical fashion, all the time she was filming *Funny Girl,* she had also been deep in pre-production telephone conferences with Ernest Lehman, producer of *Hello, Dolly!*

Barbra was well aware that many felt she was too young for the role, but it must have been a sweet kind of triumph to be offered it. *Dolly* and *Funny Girl* had opened within months of each other on Broadway, but it was *Dolly* that had swept the Tony Awards. *Funny Girl* closed after three years, while *Dolly* was still running and would ultimately rack up seven years on Broadway. Now the much-loved star of *Dolly,* Carol Channing, had been passed over in favor of Barbra.

Barbra acknowledged that at twenty-six she was a little young for the role of a middle-aged widow. "I thought they were kidding," she said. "I didn't want to do it. I told them not to hire me." Producer Ernest Lehman disagreed. "I'm not implying criticism of anyone else who has done the role previously, but I chose Miss Streisand because I'm convinced she's one of the most exciting talents to come along in the recent past and I know she'll be perfect for the role."

That April 10, only days before she was due to begin *Dolly,* Barbra appeared at the Academy Awards at the Santa Monica Civic Auditorium, to present the Oscar for Best Song. She announced that the winner was Leslie Bricusse for "Talk to the Animals" and that Sammy Davis, Jr. would accept for the absent songwriter. Some observers noticed a coolness in her attitude to Davis; later he confided to columnist James Bacon that he was mystified about it. It apparently had something to do with Barbra's being barred from The Factory, an exclusive private disco where Davis was a member of the board of directors, but he claimed to know nothing about it.

"I SAY 'TO HELL WITH YOU,' AND SHE SAYS, 'TO HELL WITH YOU!' WE'RE PERFECTLY MATCHED"

Cameras started rolling April 15, 1968 and they were committed to a tight ninety-day shooting schedule. Barbra had chosen Gene Kelly to direct. Although Kelly himself was best known as a dancer, another choreographer, Michael Kidd, was brought in as dance director. Kelly emerged from his preproduction meetings with Barbra impressed with her professionalism and dedication. "She's a worker and an indefatigable trouper," he said. "I found her attack exciting. Many actors concentrate solely on their performances. Barbra does this, but she also wants to know what the effect will be."

But unfortunately, Barbra had her doubts about Kelly, doubts she kept to herself at the time. Later she would reveal how distressed she had been when she asked him about his cinematic concept of the musical and he didn't have one. He never saw the possibilities. According to Ernest Lehman, Barbra lost confidence in Kelly when he could not help her with her interpretation of her role.

Kelly, in turn, felt she did not recognize his status as a musical and dance veteran. He blamed their problems on the tight schedule. "If only there had been more time, I'd have tried to help her work out a clear-cut characterization," Kelly told his biographer, Clive Hirschhorn. "But we had a tight schedule and I left it up to her. The result was she was being Mae West one minute, Fanny Brice the other, and Barbra Streisand the next. Her accent varied as much as her mannerisms. She kept experimenting with new things out of sheer desperation, none of which really worked to her satisfaction. And as she's such a perfectionist, she became neurotic and insecure."

"I thought it could have been a wild film," she said ruefully. With *Funny Girl* not yet released, Barbra was very much aware that she was carrying the responsibility for this multi-million dollar picture. "If this were your second film, and there was a fortune backing it, how would you feel?" she asked one reporter. "Everyone expects me to behave like a star, but deep down I hate having to smile when I don't want to, to hide what I really feel."

Walter Matthau was co-starring as Horace Vandergelder, Dolly's suitor. Others in the cast included Tommy Tune, who played Ambrose Kemper, the frustrated suitor of Horace Vandergelder's niece, and Michael Crawford, as Vandergelder's employee, Cornelius. Everyone suffered through rigorous location shoots at Garrison, Cold Springs, and West Point, New York, that July. On the bright side, Barbra didn't have to be in almost every scene, as she had to with *Funny Girl*.

But Matthau loathed her and made no secret of it. One particular incident had him telling her "Nobody in this company likes you." On May 20, a piece by Joyce Haber appeared in *New York* magazine, describing Barbra as a "girl monster."

Barbra clashed with Walter Matthau from the beginning.

Matthau claimed that he took the part "to build up my salary," but admitted that "there was a strange kind of attraction to the fact I was going to work with Streisand. I almost knew that I was going to blow up at her." He insisted he had tried "very hard, very hard" to be civil to her, but it was "extraordinarily difficult." "See, she's a soloist, and she likes to tell the conductor when the flutes come in, when the violins come in. When she acts—and I say that in quotes—she likes to tell the director when the other actors should come in." To Matthau, this was overstepping her boundaries. "She should simply be the instrument of the director, and not be the conductor, the composer, the scene designer, the costume designer, the acting coach, et cetera," he said.

"Unfortunately that's what happens when people become stars before they learn their craft."

Their bad feelings went back to 1965 when Barbra dropped in backstage to visit Piper Laurie at a revival of *The Glass Menagerie*. Matthau also poked his head in, spotted Barbra and said mischievously, "Oh, you must be Barbara Harris. You ought to get that nose fixed." Barbra, who has never been known for her sense of humor, claimed, "I was so shocked, I couldn't even answer him." (Matthau claims that what he actually said was: "Oh, you're Barbara Harris. I see you've had your nose done.")

During the production he took to referring to her as "Madame Ptomaine," and she called him "Old Sewer-Mouth." She even acknowledged to *Women's Wear Daily* that she missed working with Omar Sharif: "He is very conscientious and always a gentleman. He is never petty or like a vain actor. And he's always a man."

Matthau complained to another reporter that, "She steps on

your head and your tail. She's gotta wave her goddarn feathers across your balls and in your eyes, otherwise she's not happy."

They limited contact when they were not in a scene together, but in their few verbal skirmishes, Matthau seemed to come off the winner. *Esquire* reported that Barbra asked Matthau one day, "How's your ulcer?"

"I don't have an ulcer," he replied.

"My maid said she heard on the radio that I was giving you an ulcer."

"You may be giving me another heart attack, darling," said Matthau, "but not an ulcer."

Finally, Matthau grew so unhappy and convinced that the director and producer were on Barbra's side that he went to Fox head Richard Zanuck. "I'd like to help you out," Zanuck replied, "but the film is not called *'Hello, Walter!'* "

To Matthau, the trouble was that Barbra had become a star before she became an actress. He hated making the picture and developed all kinds of physical symptoms. He claims he was in agony most of the time. "All I remember and know is that I was appalled by every move she made," he says. He was outraged when she told Kelly how he should feed her lines.

The showdown came when Barbra insisted that a scene could be improved while Matthau and Kelly were satisfied. Kelly finally gave in, to the fury of Matthau. "Everybody in this company hates you!" he declared. "All right, walk off! Just remember, Betty Hutton once thought she was indispensable," Matthau jeered.

In spite of the feuding co-stars, *Dolly* was completed in late August, ahead of schedule.

Later, she speculated that the veteran felt threatened by her. "It was like he was this pro and I was this kid who didn't have any right to any opinions," she complained. It's possible Matthau and others in the Hollywood community resented her arrival with a four-picture deal.

But Ernest Lehman would remain fond of Barbra. When she was feted by the Friars Club in 1969, he wrote the souvenir program titled "Who Needs Her?" In it he poked fun at Barbra's idiosyncracies, like picking food from his plate. "What kind of behavior is this?" he wrote. "And then one day she DOESN'T eat off your plate and you get depressed. It's ridiculous." He mentioned her late-night phone calls to discuss the picture: "But to talk to him for an HOUR? . . . TWO hours? . . . just to make a few scenes BETTER? . . . just to make the WHOLE PICTURE better?

"THE ENTERTAINMENT EVENT OF THE YEAR"

Following the assassinations of Martin Luther King that March and Robert F. Kennedy that June, the show business community united on July 26 for a Hollywood Bowl concert designed to raise money for Dr. King's Poor People's Campaign. The "Entertainment Event of the Year," as it was billed, drew 18,000 people and was hosted by Bill Cosby, but the star was Barbra Streisand, who took time off from filming to perform there.

On September 16, the much-awaited *Funny Girl* opened with the largest box office advance in history, two-million dollars in advance ticket sales. Columbia backed the picture with a $1.6 million advertising and promotion campaign that included *Funny Girl* wristwatches that became instant collectors' items. The premiere was part of a gala $100–a-ticket benefit for New York Mayor John Lindsay's Commission on Youth and Physical Fitness. Barbra arrived in a directoir's wig, and a sheer silver-net rhinestone-studded gown by Arnold Scaasi.

It was Barbra's first movie premiere. "It was so exciting to go to an opening night and not be nervous and have to worry. I always envied my friends the fact that they could get dressed up and go to my openings while I had to worry and work. Now, I can go to the theater and watch myself work."

The film was followed by a party in a transparent tent in Times Square so fans could get a view of the stars. Mayor Lindsay introduced her by saying: "It's a long way from Brooklyn to Broadway." Barbra replied: "It's not so long if you take the BMT and change at Canal Street." But Barbra and Elliott were never really at ease in such a crowd and quickly slipped away.

Elliott was off to Hollywood to begin rehearsals for *Bob & Carol & Ted & Alice*. A few days later, Barbra flew out to join him for the West Coast premiere of *Funny Girl*. It opened October 9 at the Egyptian Theatre, followed by another party to benefit Cedars-Sinai Hospital. Guests ranged from Jack Benny to Diana Ross. More relaxed this time, she and Elliott lingered on until one in the morning.

Funny Girl had opened to raves, but she was determined to make it perfect. She confided that she was still hoping to get a certain musical scene restored. "I really don't think about reviews. I'm hoping to change things in the movie now. I'm hoping to add—thank God they may do it—the whole Swan Lake number. I think it's important to get something right—just for yourself."

"Now perhaps that my movie is out, they don't have to create stories, now they can talk about constructive things like my *work*. I read these things about the press being barred from seeing me and it is a bunch of crap."

But she was pleased by Pauline Kael's review of *Funny Girl* in *The New Yorker:* "The message of Barbra Streisand in *Funny Girl* is that talent is beauty."

And she bragged, "I just got a note from Hedy Lamarr, one of the most beautiful women in the world, and she said I made Elizabeth Taylor look like an old bag.

"You know, I look good in the movie. It is nobody else's

face but mine. I did my own makeup. I wear the same makeup on the street every day. No tricks, no pasting on lashes. Believe me, everything shows on the series, close.

"I'm amused when I read that I am a throwback to the stars of the '20s, when they were supposed to be temperamental and throw tantrums, and I don't know whether to laugh or cry. Anyone who knows his craft or is worth his salt and his sensitivity and intelligence doesn't throw tantrums. To have *temperament*, to be able to get angry and to cry, to be vulnerable to examination is a terrific thing. But negative temperament is childish nonsense."

Barbra never forgot or forgave. Years after *Funny Girl* wrapped, she was still angry with Wyler about one scene. "Willy Wyler really screwed up one musical number in *Funny Girl*," she told Frank Pierson, her director on *A Star is Born*, "it was the one number he had to involve himself in. His ego got in the way, he couldn't let it alone." But the person she really blamed was Ray Stark. "I had an arrangement with Ray Stark—he let me go in after and re-edit the sequence; he promised he'd put it in the TV version, but he didn't do it, the son of a bitch. It's still wrong. The director got it backwards.

"I can't stand for someone to tell me what to do," Barbra told Pierson. "Ray Stark always used to bully me, the son of a bitch. I made him and he made millions from me, millions!

"You'll pay," she warned Pierson, "for every lousy thing Ray Stark ever did to me."

"IT'S LIKE THE THEME OF FUNNY GIRL—WE LOVE EACH OTHER BUT LOVE IS NOT ENOUGH"

But Barbra and Stark could put aside their differences for the sake of the film they both cared so much about. Stark always publicly defended his star. "She has a basic truth within herself that can stand the miserable analysis of being amplified five-hundred times on the big screen." As for her reported lateness, he explained she just had no sense of time. What did a few lost minutes matter, anyway, when you were working with an artist?

As for charges by former model Carolyn Kenmore and co-star Anne Francis that Barbra had cut their parts out of jealousy, Stark insisted that she had nothing to do with it.

He acknowledged that their relationship was sometimes strained. "It's like the theme of *Funny Girl*," he explained. "We love each other, but love is not enough."

Ray Stark found her "warmer, gentler, more considerate and mature," than she had been during the play. He marveled at how she could be herself and succeed in Hollywood among the "barracudas."

Fall of 1968 found Barbra comfortable with her superstardom and her professionalism. She was no longer a mere phenomenon; it was becoming clear that she was here to stay.

Little Jason Emanuel, twenty-one months old, had become a familiar figure on the sets of *Funny Girl* and *Hello, Dolly!* "I called her up this week to read her the greatest review I had read about anyone in my life," a press agent said. "Her maid told me she couldn't answer just now because she was giving the baby a bath."

"He's incredible, an incredible little human being, a great joy. The only real contribution I will make to this world," said Barbra.

She was also busy denying rumors that her marriage was in trouble. "He's very bright and sensitive," she said of Elliott. "Totally non-opportunistic about my career. It would have been a problem a long time ago. Maybe the beginning, if he lived through that . . ." He had just finished *Minsky's*, but there came a point when he was so desperate he called on Mike Frankovich, head of production at Columbia Pictures.

"Mike," he said, "I want to go into production. I want to be your assistant."

Frankovich recalled the meeting in his office for a visitor: "I looked at this hairy Jewish boy and I thought, 'What does this guy want to go into production for?' I had a script on my desk called *Bob & Carol & Ted & Alice*. I impulsively threw it at him. I told him to take the script home and read it. I said, 'I want you in this movie. If, after you read the script, you still want to get out of acting, then we'll talk about your going into production." Frankovich went on, "The next day he called and said he wanted to do the movie. The rest, of course is beautiful history." That picture would make Elliott, for a time, the most sought-after actor in Hollywood.

But the stress of waiting for that big break while his wife's star shone brighter each day was starting to get to Elliott. That October 28, photographer Tony Rizzo claimed that he had been attacked "and flung across the sidewalk" by Elliott while he was taking pictures of Elliott and Barbra outside the Directors Guild of America Theater where the couple had attended a preview of *Bullit*.

UCLA Medical Center confirmed that Rizzo had received treatment in the hospital's emergency room and police said he had made a battery report.

A month later, Rizzo filed suit for more than $200,000 for damages he claimed he suffered from the so-called beating, alleging that Elliott "willfully and violently struck him," while he was performing his job.

In fact, Barbra and Elliott claimed that Rizzo's flashbulbs had been exploding in their face all evening and Barbra asked him to stop. When Elliott asked "Haven't you got enough yet?" Rizzo responded: "Sir, if you were polite and stopped walking like everyone else, we wouldn't have to bother you now." With that an angry Elliott lunged at him, shouting "I'll show you who is not polite, I'll break your camera, you son of a bitch!" The photographer continued to jeer at him: "Watch your mouth—there are ladies present."

Barbra fled with their friend Abbe Lane, but the next day the incident was widely reported in the press. By the time the case went to trial, the Goulds would be divorced, but Barbra testified for her ex-husband. Elliott insisted, "I never struck or hit him in any way. I was very careful to put him down as gently as I could." After a two-day non-jury trial in June 1971, the judge dismissed Rizzo's claims of assault and battery but did award him $6,500 for his "manhandling," then asked Elliott for his autograph.

This marked the beginning of an interesting motif in Barbra's life: to love her was to clash with the press. Elliott was the first to go *mano a mano* with photographers, but in the future Jon Peters, Don Johnson, and Andre Agassi would be among the lovers who would battle with lensmen who got too close.

Barbra's best friends were still her oldest friends. That included Cis and Dr. Harvey Corman, and, most especially, Marty Erlichman. "Other people love money," Barbra said, "but Marty loves me."

And, of course, Elliott. "He does it so great with me but I can't begin to do it for him," she confided to journalist Liz Smith. "To me he is a mixture of Bogart, the Michelangelo statue of David and—Jean-Paul Belmondo."

"Does he take care of you?" Smith asked.

"Yeah," Barbra said softly. "Yeah, he sure does."

Nine

Elliott Gets His Chance

"Barbra is really fourteen years old. Her problem is not only that she has been swept off her feet by phenomenal success. It is more than that. . . . If Barbra conquers the world, if every last person in it says, 'Barbra Streisand, you are the most beautiful, intelligent person, the greatest,' it will be the saddest thing for her. Finally, she is going to be left with herself. She will have to look herself in the eye and say: 'I have got to find out for myself.' "

—Elliott Gould

The year 1969 started with more rumors of trouble between Barbra and Elliott. Gossip columnist Earl Wilson reported that "Barbra Streisand and her husband are having marriage problems. The problems are personal and neither will discuss them. But they're further apart now than the mere mileage that separates them."

January 6, filming began on Barbra's third big-budget musical, *On a Clear Day You Can See Forever.* Shortly before production began producer Howard Koch and lyricist Alan Jay Lerner launched it with the memorable Reincarnation Ball,

January 3, at the Beverly Hilton. Five hundred Hollywood notables were invited to attend, in costume, disguised as "anybody in world history you might like to have been in a previous lifetime."

Barbra's future in town was still uncertain and consequently most of the A-list celebrities did not show up. Still, there was Phyllis Diller as Kim Novak, Polly Bergen as Queen Elizabeth I, Barbara Parkins as Eliza Doolittle, Omar Sharif as Che Guevara, and Tony Curtis as himself.

With music by Burton Lane and lyrics by Alan Jay Lerner, *On a Clear Day* had run for 280 performances on Broadway but had never become the musical comedy institution that *Dolly* and *Funny Girl* had. Paramount acquired the movie rights for $750,000 in 1966 and producer Howard Koch immediately went after the most important young musical star around. Barbra, who was appearing in *Funny Girl* in London at the time, turned him down. After several false starts, Koch finally managed to get Barbra aboard by giving her advance approval of the creative team. She requested Vincente Minelli to direct because she had always admired *Gigi*, his 1958 film. She wanted Cecil Beaton for her period costumes and Arnold Scaasi for her contemporary clothes, and finally, she asked for Harry Stradling because he had already photographed her so beautifully for *Funny Girl* and *Dolly*.

On a Clear Day may have also appealed to Barbra because it was not a traditional (read: old-fashioned) musical like *Dolly* and *Funny Girl*. It was much more a play with music with some serious dramatic themes. In fact, after the opening number, there are no songs for thirty minutes into the film. She would be playing a contemporary woman, Daisy Gamble, who sees a therapist, played in the movie by Yves Montand, because her fiancé insists she give up smoking. With Daisy under hypnosis, Montand unearths her past lives which include a Regency aristocrat, Melinda.

Playing a dual role appealed to Barbra. She had seen the musical on Broadway and considered it "heaven, just heaven. The two parts are close to my schizophrenic personality," she said. "They appeal to the frightened girl and the strong woman in me."

Lerner and Lane wrote new material especially for Barbra, including "E.S.P.," a lavish production number in which Daisy appears in all her previous lives, speaking French, Italian, Spanish, German, and English, but it was cut from the picture because of budget constraints.

The creative team soon grew used to Barbra's perfectionism. "She'll never just say, 'Oh, I suppose that's all right, let's go out to dinner.' It's a constant battle of attrition with her and her taste—which is very exhausting," Cecil Beaton told a reporter from *Look* magazine. As for Howard Koch, he thrived on her demands: "Working with Barbra Streisand is like making love. She'll know twenty different ways of doing a scene, and it's so much fun finding the right way." A week after filming began, Barbra took a ten-day leave to fly to Europe for the French and British premieres of *Funny Girl.* (She had originally campaigned to dub the European versions herself, until Columbia executives convinced her that not even Barbra Streisand could learn the thirteen-song score in French, German, and Italian in three months.) In London, at a post-screening dinner party with H.R.H. Princess Margaret, David Frost and Ray Stark, among others, Barbra met the next important man in her life: Canadian Premier Pierre Elliott Trudeau.

Returning to the set of *On a Clear Day,* Barbra was teamed for a duet with a then-unknown Jack Nicholson who played her ex-stepbrother. *Easy Rider* had not yet been released, and Nicholson took the part mainly because he needed money. But he has fond memories of working with Barbra: "Streisand treated me great, man," he recalls. "I don't think she saw *Easy*

Rider either, so it wasn't because of that. She tried to help in my scenes, you know?"

"WE'RE NO LONGER TRYING TO SAVE OUR MARRIAGE."

At last, it looked as if Elliott's career was about to take off. *The Night They Raided Minsky's* had received some good reviews and he was about to begin filming at Columbia in *Bob & Carol & Ted & Alice,* a movie about the new morality and the young married middle class that seemed tailor-made for him. Elliott would play a straight-arrow lawyer married to Dyan Cannon, with Robert Culp an architect married to Natalie Wood.

But that February, 1969, Lee Solters, Barbra's publicist, released an announcement that they were splitting up. "We're no longer trying to save our marriage," Elliott said. "What we've saved is a nice working relationship which we didn't have before."

"It's an age-old theme," Barbra acknowledged later. In fact, it was a theme she would later explore in *A Star is Born,* but that didn't make it any less painful. Elliott had cared about her before she was a star and he had stayed by her side during the first hectic years after *Wholesale.*

Perhaps Barbra's fling with Omar Sharif had more impact on them than either wanted to acknowledge. It certainly sounds as if Elliott had the relationship in mind when he discussed his separation with columnist Joyce Haber: "Actors dress for effect," he told her. "Actors date for effect. It all suddenly becomes real to them and they're affected."

Later, Barbra would be able to say "I think our divorce freed him. Freed his creativity, too. It also made him more ambitious, which I felt was a good thing for him."

The couple was still joined by mutual interests, their love for their son and their business partnerships. Barbra told *Mod-*

ern Screen, "I'll be associated with him in a producing capacity on the three pictures he is going to make on a new Universal contract. We'll consult on everything from buying properties to the actual casting." As for any other details, Barbra was not talking. "Beyond that, what has happened is between Elliott and me, not the curious," she told *Modern Screen.* "We have to find out how things are between us and the less outside influence, the better."

"HELLO, GORGEOUS!"

At about the same time that Barbra was announcing her separation from Elliott, the Motion Picture Academy of Arts and Sciences was announcing nominations for the 1969 awards. Barbra was nominated for Best Actress, along with Katharine Hepburn (*The Lion in Winter*), Patricia Neal (*The Subject Was Roses*), Vanessa Redgrave (*Isadora*), and Joanne Woodward (*Rachel, Rachel*).

Among such an illustrious line-up, Barbra was considered a dark horse. Joanne Woodward and Katharine Hepburn were the favorites. Each had accumulated a strong body of work and the love and admiration of her peers. Barbra, on the other hand, was still a brash and controversial newcomer who had already alienated some of the most powerful people in the motion picture community.

Barbra's natural shyness took over and she was reluctant to show how much she wanted to win that Oscar. It was up to Ray Stark and Columbia Pictures to campaign relentlessly for her with multiple ads in the trade papers and a lavish schedule of screenings and parties.

"We had screenings and elaborate supper parties every night," a Columbia publicist recalls. "It was an opportunity for her to meet the voters. Finally she decided to show, but only after she called me to check out what was on the dinner menu. We had three different entrees—chicken cordon bleu, prime rib, and quiche with salad. She would have none of that. Barbra ordered her own menu for a party of five, and then she never showed."

That April 14, the night of the Academy Awards ceremony at the Dorothy Chandler pavilion, Barbra donned see-through black tulle evening pajamas by Scaasi with a white Peter Pan collar and sleeves. Wearing one of the seventeen wigs designed by Fred Glaser for her role in *Clear Day,* Barbra gave the public a sneak peak at the Daisy Gamble look: a page boy gone mad. Later, Glaser complained to Streisand biographer Shaun Considine that Barbra had pressed him to make the wig fuller, as teased and raised as possible. "I kept telling her it looked overdone, phony," he recalled, "and she said, 'Good!' The whole town is phony, and if I lose they'll know I don't give a damn.' "

Barbra sat with her estranged husband by her side as Ingrid Bergman announced the winner: it was a tie: Katharine Hepburn and Barbra Streisand.

"I heard one name," Barbra recalled, "then another. I wasn't sure if it was mine until Elly turned to me and said, 'It's you.' "

As a trembling Barbra walked to the stage, her heel caught in the hem of her couture pajamas. "For two thousand dollars they can't sew the goddamn thing," she muttered. But by the time she reached the podium she had pulled herself together. She grabbed her gold statuette and, grinning broadly, said, "Hello, gorgeous," instantly winning over the audience. After all the rumors and buzz and bad press, these insiders and pillars of the Hollywood establishment were seeing the real Barbra, the down-to-earth girl from Brooklyn who acknowledged the greatness of her co-winner, Katharine Hepburn, and broke into sincere tears at her own good fortune.

"I was amazed," recalled one observer. "We expected her to be bold and brash as always, but when she began to cry I thought, 'Well, she's not so tough after all, she does have feelings.' "

"I'm very honored to be in such magnificent company as Katharine Hepburn," she said, once she got control of herself. "Gee whiz, it's kind of a wild feeling. Sitting here tonight, I was thinking that the first script of *Funny Girl* was written when I was only eleven years old. Thank God it took so long to get it right, you know?"

After thanking her colleagues, she ended with "Somebody once said to me, asked me if I was happy and I said, 'Are you kidding? I'd be miserable if I was happy.' And I'd like to thank all the members of the Academy for making me *really* miserable. Thank you."

To outsiders it might have looked as if Barbra and Elliott were going to reconcile, but that was out of the question. They were headed in two different directions. In fact, Elliott loathed the whole Hollywood scene and only came to the Oscar ceremony to support Barbra.

"The year I took Barbra to the Academy Awards and she won her Oscar, I smoked some grass beforehand," he told Richard Warren Lewis of *Playboy*. He disliked formal black tie events. He was also terribly self-conscious about being with a woman from whom he had just separated and about being among people he felt weird about, people who thrived on the dramatic implications of such a situation. He went to give support to Barbra, with whom he was still quite friendly, but he was ambivalent about what he was trying to prove and to whom. "It was a difficult night for me—a trauma," he acknowledged.

LITTLE SISTER

Just a week after Barbra's Academy Award triumph, her stepfather Louis Kind passed away in obscurity. A year earlier, her half-sister, Roslyn Kind, had released an album of her own, *Give Me You* with RCA and even appeared on *The Ed Sullivan Show* to promote it. She had a two-week engagement at the Hungry i in San Francisco.

HONORS

That May 16, Barbra was feted by the Friars Club of New York as Entertainer of the Year, the first woman so honored since Sophie Tucker. The gala was held at the Grand Ballroom of the Waldorf-Astoria. William Wyler was working and unable to make it, but he sent a telegraph: "As your co-director on *Funny Girl* I became so accustomed to relying on your suggestions as to how the picture should be made that I am very much at a loss now that I must go it alone again. Congratulations. 'Entertainer of the Year' is an honor you have earned and along with it, in my opinion, 'Director of the Year.' "

POWER

By June, *Clear Day* had wrapped. Barbra had now completed three big-budget films and she had learned a lot about Hollywood power and how to use it. She had been negotiating with Paul Newman and Sidney Poitier, all fellow clients of David Begelman and Freddie Fields of CMA, to create a production company of their own. On June 11, Newman, Poitier, and Streisand announced the formation of their partnership, First Artists. Each of the three partners would make a total of three pictures; each would select his or her own projects, which were not to exceed $3 million in budgets, except for musicals which could go to $5 million. The artists were responsible for development, production, and editing. They received no salary, but had final cut and a percentage of the gross. The three founders were soon joined by Steve McQueen and Dustin Hoffman.

This was not a totally original venture. They were actually creating a modern version of First Artists, the production company formed by Mary Pickford, Douglas Fairbanks, and Charlie Chaplin in the 1920's.

LAS VEGAS

On July 2, Barbra opened the International Hotel's Showroom Internationale in Las Vegas, billed as "The Most Exciting Star in the World." She was drawing a reported $1 million for a four-week engagement, but according to Marty Erlichman, it wasn't the money ($100,000 a week plus stock options), that drew Barbra but the excitement of Las Vegas. There was also the opportunity to promote her three movies.

Unfortunately, things went wrong from the start. Delays in shooting *On a Clear Day* cut into her rehearsal time. Days before the scheduled opening, the Showroom was still unfinished. At the International's request, Barbra and Erlichman attended other acts in town, but Barbra was horrified when she saw a heckler forcibly ejected from Dean Martin's show. She feared she would have to deal with the same kind of pest. "If they do that to him," she wondered, "what will they do to me?"

By now, Barbra admitted, she was used to the cocoon-like world of movie-making, yet she forced herself to go through with Las Vegas to prove that she was not tied to one medium.

Barbra's Vegas appearance was supposed to be a big event, not just because of her star status, but because it was the opening of a glittering new hotel. A flotilla of Hollywood stars and celebrities, among them Cary Grant, Natalie Wood, Rudolf Nureyev, Andy Williams, George Raft, and Peggy Lee, were flown in especially for her opening night. For the girl from Brooklyn it was supposed to be a dream come true.

Instead, Barbra's opening night was a nightmare. Most of the hotel rooms were not ready for occupancy and guests were diverted to the Flamingo instead. Wet paint, inadequate air conditioning, leaking water from a pool on the floor above, and poor sound quality were only a few of the indignities that guests and star were subjected to that night.

Barbra's act was not terribly different from the act she brought to Vegas in 1963, except that it now included songs from her three movies. Her approach was still no-frills, unless you counted her jewelled microphone. She disdained back-up singers, dancers, a warm-up act or costume changes, all those staples of the Vegas clubs. In a raspberry chiffon gown, she joked, "This was my bedspread. Just thought I'd put it on and make a costume!" Her audience was not amused.

In the days that followed, most of her critics focused on her lack of small talk. A particularly negative *Hollywood Reporter* review acknowledged her voice but was otherwise merciless:

"Barbra Streisand is very fortunate indeed to be making a reputed $100,000 a week, at the posh new International Hotel. Now she can afford to get someone to write an act for her. It would be money well spent. Her voice, a remarkable instrument about which enough has been said . . . came through fine. But never does she warm up to the people nor they to her. The sameness of arrangements, the sameness of the treatment she gives each song, makes for such monotony, you can't believe. A real live Barbie Doll." The reviewer also noted that there was no standing ovation.

The next day Barbra admitted, "I don't enjoy working in front of a bunch of strangers." Later, in fact, she confided to *Los Angeles Times* critic Charles Champlin that the experience brought back the stage fright she had incurred during the run of *Funny Girl* on Broadway. "I'd hear myself doing the lines or singing but it was like hearing a stranger," she said. "It drove me into analysis."

Audience members complained that Barbra was aloof, unaware that she was actually almost paralyzed with fear. Sadly, she felt no love from the audience, telling Champlin: "You could feel the hostility of the opening night audience, all the gamblers who were there because they're important to the hotel, all the actors who resent the fact that you're doing things they think they should be doing. It's total fear time up there. I don't enjoy performing before a bunch of strangers. I don't care about pleasing a group. Some performers get a thrill out of winning over a cold audience—I talked to Elvis about it last night. He does—I don't. It turns me off."

She kept asking herself, what was she supposed to be? She later told the *Los Angeles Herald-Examiner:* "The moment I stepped on stage I was in shock. It was like 'what am I doing here?' "

The opening night audience was unaware of another episode that had devastated Barbra just before she went on stage. It was while preparing in her dressing room that she learned of a devastatingly negative article in the August *Ladies Home Journal,* an article all the more painful because it was Elliott discussing their relationship and the collapse of their marriage.

Her former hair stylist Freddy Glaser told Streisand biographer Shaun Considine that someone mentioned it casually just a half hour before showtime. "Barbra knew nothing about the article," said Glaser, "and I'm thinking, *Please, let her be, I have to get her ready for tonight's show.* But they kept it going, until she sent five people running in different directions to get the magazine. When she read it she cleared everyone from the room. She proceeded to tear the place apart. I tried to calm her down. I had to get her ready. She had these elaborate hairpieces I had to fix on her head. It was impossible. She wouldn't stand still."

It's small wonder that Barbra was upset. Much of what he said surely hurt, but the most painful thing must have been the idea that he had talked to the press at all. But Elliott believed that the reporter had wronged him as much as Barbra.

According to him, shortly after he and Barbra separated, he sat down for what he thought was a chat with a friend. Now he found his most intimate feelings part of an article in *Ladies' Home Journal*. He was outraged, although he did not deny the accuracy of the quotes.

"Barbra and I were like a lot of unhappy married couples," he had told the *Journal*'s Diana Lurie. "We could have gone on living together for another ten years and never reconciled our problems. For years we talked sporadically about separating. We threatened it, and we even tried it, but the two of us were always so inhibited and insecure that we came back to each other."

Elliott acknowledged that the separation was difficult and painful, but he was much happier since it happened.

"I don't think Barbra can help me," he said. "Barbra is really fourteen years old. Her problem is not only that she has been swept off her feet by phenomenal success. It is more than that. It is what she thinks about herself. If Barbra conquers the world, if every last person in it says, 'Barbra Streisand, you are the most beautiful, intelligent person, the greatest,' it will be the saddest thing for her. Finally, she is going to be left with herself. She will have to look herself in the eye and say: 'I have got to find out for myself.' "

Elliott claimed that "Barbra's favorite subject is Barbra." And he insisted that he did not envy her and he did not resent being called "Mr. Streisand." He also complained about the rumors that Barbra had invested $100,000 to mount his Broadway flop, *Drat! the Cat!,* when all they had invested was a total of $750 apiece.

For Elliott, the most difficult thing about their separation was its effect on their son. "We are both concerned about Jason," he acknowledged, expressing that it troubled him to think of Jason growing up in a house of women.

And Elliott had some interesting insights into Barbra's relationships with men in general. "One side of Barbra needed me," he said. "The other was disdainful of men—and competitive toward them. Barbra has ambivalent feelings about men. She wants to be attractive to them, but is afraid she isn't. She has a problem that she can't reconcile—that men are no good and can't be trusted."

Although the days of the Hansel and Gretel of Third Avenue were over, Elliott was still enormously fond of her. "She is still that scared, shy, vulnerable girl." And he still held out hope for a reconciliation. "Barbra and I might get together again," he told Lurie. "Possibly. Nothing would please me more. . . . People who genuinely care about Barbra and me would like us to make it. But, honestly speaking, I doubt if we will."

Perhaps in an effort at damage control, Elliott showed up to see Barbra's act at the International. The bond between them was still strong and he clearly regretted causing her pain, even inadvertently. "We're great friends—but not pals," he said. "We can be even more honest and close professionally than we were before. Though we are not close personally, we still have great respect for each other. We've cut away a lot of that misunderstanding that is caused by the convention of marriage, which obliges you to continue a relationship that is obviously in a rut."

Elliott also vehemently denied that career problems caused their break-up. "The fact that Barbra was a celebrity had nothing to do with it," he insisted. "Her stardom is extraordinary, but a taxi driver could encounter the same problems we had."

PIERRE TRUDEAU

Now that Barbra was officially separated, there were rumors of a romance with Warren Beatty, but far more serious was her romance that fall with Canadian Prime Minister Pierre Elliott Trudeau. By the end of the year Barbra's relationship with the dashing head of state was serious indeed. He escorted her to the Arts Center in Ottawa and jumped from his limousine to open her door.

Barbra reportedly gave serious thought to marrying Trudeau. It would have meant learning French, basing her career in Canada, but ultimately she believed that "his life was too important to a whole country, to a world."

ELLIOTT ON THE COVER OF *TIME* MAGAZINE

That fall, Elliott's latest film, *Bob & Carol & Ted & Alice,* was already starting to look like a winner and it hadn't even officially opened yet. He had been perfectly cast as the bumbling but mostly faithful lawyer Ted who briefly succumbs to an affair while away from home.

The early inside word on *Bob & Carol & Ted & Alice* was so strong that Elliott was soon cast in three more major films back-to-back: In *M*A*S*H* he would play a zany Army surgeon; and in *Move* he walked dogs, had wild sexual fantasies, and wrote pornography. But it was *Getting Straight* that would probably generate the most controversy. Producer-director Richard Rush, who cast Elliott as a hip, articulate graduate student trying to get his master's degree in the middle of a campus riot, said: "Elliott is the most talented, versatile, imaginative actor I have come across. He has an incredible range."

Taking a short break between filming *Getting Straight* and *Move,* he told a reporter that he did not feel he had to live in Barbra's shadow while they were together. "If anything, living so close to Barbra's success has helped me to understand certain values. It's helped me to deal with my success very realistically, and not to be seduced into thinking that it is the ultimate thing."

Suddenly, Elliott's career was red-hot. His shaggy good looks seemed to destine him for the prototype of the 1970s film star. He seemed on the threshold of a career to equal Barbra's. And, like Barbra, he was eager to diversify. "The kind of heat that is developing in my career can be very helpful to the production company I have," he said. "I'll develop properties for myself, although it wasn't formed for me to act. I also hope to direct."

When he was on the cover of *Time* magazine that fall, Barbra could only be happy. "It was fabulous," she said. "I was very proud of him. I wanted it very much for him and for my son."

"I'm the hottest thing in Hollywood right now," he said that October. "By the end of the year, I'll have made four movies. Four movies in one year—that's not bad, right? I always knew there were things going on in me, that I had something to express."

And he insisted that he and Barbra were the best of friends. "Whenever Barbra and I see each other," he said, "she sings 'Happy Days are Here Again' and I break into an old tap dance. Maybe we'll get back together again, maybe we won't. I know that I'll never take her out in public again, like I did to the Academy Awards last spring. When I see her now, we go to little out-of-the way places where no one sees us."

He did not believe that his making it so big would cause any major changes in their relationship. "I'm not trying to compete with her," he insisted. "She's the most talented person I've ever known or seen. I think she's really pleased with my success. She said she liked me in *Bob & Carol,* and she has terrific taste, and if she says something's good, then it is. What I really want for her is to be as happy as I would like to be. And right now I'm happy. I'm sort of on my Odyssey.

"What we've saved is our relationship. What we've gotten is a nice working relationship, which we didn't have before. My friends ask me if I think I'm a better actor now that we've separated. I think I'd be a jerk to say yes. I made *Bob & Carol* while I was still living with Barbra. That was the direct breakthrough or the emanation of my success."

Elliott enjoyed every minute of it. "I don't take the success seriously, though. But I'm pleased for my friends. There are a lot of people I want to be able to help—actors, writers, and directors. And now I'm finally in a position to."

Elliott was doubtful that he would get married again. "I'm not against marriage," he insisted. "I want to have other kids. But I really don't like women. I mean, I'm attracted to them, but I don't want to be friends with them. I don't want to have a woman for a pal."

WHAT ABOUT TODAY?

While Elliott was briefly becoming the movie embodiment of their generation, Barbra's success was cutting her off from it. She was so committed to her work that colleagues wondered how much she even knew about the world outside the sound stage and the recording studio. Sometimes, when they actually found out, the truth could come as a shock.

There was, for example, an incident during the filming of *Clear Day*. Originally, the *Clear Day* production company was scheduled to film campus scenes at Fordham University in the Bronx, but their permit was canceled after student riots at other campuses in the New York area. The company moved to UCLA to film the scenes. Earnest and curious as ever, Barbra tried to question the student extras about the reasons behind their unrest. "What are you fighting for," she asked them, "longer vacations?"

"I know nothing about the Vietnam war or about black power, or what's happening in the world today," Barbra acknowledged. "I've got this backlog of magazines to read and catch up on, but I have no time. It's not easy being me, y'know?"

This isolation from her contemporaries was beginning to affect Barbra's record sales. She was no longer the sweetheart of Columbia Records. She had been supplanted by a newcomer, Janis Joplin, who had been signed after a dazzling appearance at the historic Monterey Pop Festival. The San Francisco-based Joplin and her band, Big Brother and the Holding Company, were leaders in a new wave of music and Columbia jumped into the swim, leaving Barbra feeling slightly stranded on shore.

Barbra openly disliked most rock music, but she recognized commercial realities. Her more recent albums, *J M'Appelle Barbra, Simply Streisand, Funny Girl* (the movie soundtrack), and *A Happening in Central Park* had sold well, but nowhere near the numbers of her first few albums. And she had not had a hit single since "People" in 1964.

She and Marty Erlichman were committed to keeping her a star in *all* venues and they were not willing to let her recording career languish. With Erlichman's support, Barbra began experimenting with more contemporary material. That May she began recording a new album, *What About Today?* with a new producer, Wally Gold.

"All I remember about that [first] day is that Marty Erlichman was there, checking me out," Gold recalled for Shaun Considine. "I treated the date like any other. When she did something wrong, I stopped her in the middle of a take. Marty said 'What are you doing! *You* don't stop her, she stops you!' I didn't *know.* I did it out of instinct. And Barbra said, 'Why?'—

from her screen. She always worked with a screen around her. She hated people looking at her and it isolated her in terms of sound. When she asked how come I stopped her, I told her. It had to do with the score which I could read and she couldn't. And she said, 'Okay, let's do it from the top again!' "

DOLLY!

That December, *Hello, Dolly!* finally premiered at the Rivoli Theatre in New York. Barbra arrived in white fox and leather, escorted by Marty Erlichman. They sat for what seemed like hours in the back of Barbra's limousine, looking out in horror at the crowds, who were threatening to break down the police barricades to get at their idol.

The scene was like something out of *Day of the Locust.* The mob started rocking Barbra's car until police cleared a path and allowed her to escape. She was immediately separated from Erlichman who was attacked by an elderly woman because he accidentally blocked her camera.

"Marty! Marty!" Barbra screamed. "Are you all right?"

The premiere in Los Angeles was even wilder. On the scene were Mr. and Mrs. Ray Stark, Mr. and Mrs. Kirk Douglas, Goldie Hawn, Mitzi Gaynor, Joan Collins, Jill St. John, George Raft, and Governor and Mrs. Reagan. Walter Matthau even kissed Barbra for photographers. But reviews were uniformly negative. *Dolly* was a financial flop.

Critics got to see what happened when Barbra was not matched with a strong director. In *Funny Girl* William Wyler and, to a lesser extent, Herb Ross, had earned her trust. But *Dolly* director Gene Kelly and choreographer Michael Kidd seemed lost. *Newsweek* called *Dolly* a "slow, plodding dinosaur of a film." The critic slammed Kelly and Kidd, claiming that "Several shakily written comedy scenes are just as shakily performed because no one knew how to direct or cut them. The

"Hello, Dolly!" number comes in fits and starts because no one knew how to make it build, visually or dramatically. The forty million extras in the big parade scene look like a routine rabble because no one knew where to put the cameras."

But this picture also lacked the strong hand of Ray Stark.

PUSSYCAT

Barbra didn't pause to agonize about the perceived failure of *Dolly!* She had wrapped *Clear Day* and was characteristically already deep into her next film: *The Owl and the Pussycat.*

Like so many Hollywood projects, especially Barbra's, *Pussycat* had a long and colorful history.

Barbra had settled Ray Stark's 1967 lawsuit in part by agreeing to do another picture for him. The picture she wanted to do was a comedy, *The Owl and the Pussycat,* that she had seen on the stage in London. On Broadway it had starred Diana Sands, her old colleague from *Another Evening with Harry Stoones,* and Alan Alda.

In November 1968, it was announced that Barbra would star in *Pussycat.* The male lead, the priggish bookstore clerk, would be played by George Segal. Herb Ross would direct. But as part of the deal, Barbra had insisted that there would be absolutely no singing in the picture. This would present her as an *actress.* Some stars insist on no nudity, Barbra insisted on no singing. Ever-resourceful, Stark announced that Barbra's character, the callgirl/part-time model Doris, would, in the film, be a call girl/folk singer.

As long as *Pussycat* was a straight comedy, Barbra was enthusiastic. "It's such a shlep doing those big musicals—it takes a year, a whole lifetime away from you, rehearsing, prerecording, fittings, etc. Now I can make a little movie in ten weeks, no songs, like a normal person."

Barbra was also delighted that *Pussycat* would be filmed entirely in New York. She got along beautifully with Ross and George Segal. They found her generous, and willing to do things their way. "She has a feeling not everyone loves her," said Ross, "but that she's one of us."

At one point, the script called for a nude scene. Barbra resisted. Ross pressed her. She was self-conscious about her body—Ross assured her it was fine. "She has beautiful bosoms," he said, "and her vanity wants to show them off. On the other hand, she's a little intimidated by the whole idea. However, knowing women, I think vanity will win."

After much discussion, Barbra agreed to shoot a topless scene, then changed her mind and demanded that the scene be cut and that the film negative be given to her. Unfortunately, she did not get all of them, as she would learn to her dismay a decade later, when the magazine *High Society* published them.

The experience was clouded when illness forced her favorite cinematographer, Harry Stradling, to withdraw. (He would die the following February.) She had developed enormous respect for him. They had worked on four pictures together, and she affectionately called him "Uncle Harry." He was replaced by Andrew Laszlo, who had worked with Elliott on *Minsky's*.

Pussycat began filming in New York on October 6. Always quick to understand the importance of star perks, whether it was the free dinners in those midwestern nightclubs or a specially decorated movie star dressing room, Barbra now demanded and got a lavishly redecorated dressing room, full of white carpeting and lighted mirrors and a star on the door.

But she was never far from her past. One day Diana Kind paid a surprise visit to the set to see her daughter the movie star.

"She had on a skimpy costume and was very embarrassed when she saw me," Mrs. Kind complained. "I'm really shocked at all these things an actress has to do today. But I guess it's part of the job."

Pussycat turned out to be one of Barbra's happiest film-making experiences. According to Herb Ross, "There was a peculiar intimacy in the film with so few of us involved and we had to break down our inhibitions to do it. We rehearsed two weeks before shooting, and got so loose it was silly. . . . We lay in bed together on the set and just laughed."

POLITICAL ACTIVIST

Barbra also began to explore the role of political activist. She campaigned for George McGovern for President, for John Lindsay for Mayor of New York City, and Bella Abzug for Congresswoman.

Yet one liberal cause that Barbra never embraced was the women's movement. When the *Playboy* interviewer asked Barbra point-blank "Are you a feminist?" Barbra demurred, "I never thought about the women's movement while I was moving as a woman. I didn't even realize I was fighting this battle all the time," she said, but she acknowledged, "I now understand it in the whole picture of revolution."

DISCRIMINATION

In spite of all she had achieved, even Barbra occasionally had to face discrimination. Since separating from Elliott, she had been looking for a new place to live and she thought she found it in a twenty-room cooperative apartment on Park Avenue at 85th Street, only to be rejected by the co-op board. She was excluded in spite of a letter on her behalf from Governor Nelson Rockefeller who praised her warmly and noted that she was a quiet person, not prone to party-giving.

Although no reason for Barbra's rejection was made public

by the co-op, the wife of one of the building's board of directors said that she was turned down because she was a "flamboyant type."

For Barbra, the characterization was ironic. "I have been criticized in Hollywood for not attending premieres or giving parties, etc.

"I had thought that the mid-Victorian notion of actors as undesirables or second-class citizens was a prejudice which had gone the way of the bustle," Barbra said in her statement. "I am an actress by choice; I am proud of my profession, and I am not prepared to accept an infringement on my civil rights because of it."

She added that her present landlord had written to the co-op's board stating that "my home was never used as a rehearsal hall, nor had there been any complaints about disturbances in my present apartment building due to my presence."

Barbra also revealed that this was not the first time she had faced discrimination in housing. Only a year earlier she had attempted to buy an apartment at 1107 Fifth Avenue. "I suspect now that the reason for that refusal may well have been the same as in the present situation," she said.

Barbra was convinced the reason was at least partly because she was Jewish. That December, Barbra was seriously considering filing a complaint with New York City's Commission on Human Rights.

"I have been looking for an apartment in New York City for some three years," she said in a written statement. "Immediately agents eliminated specific buildings from my consideration, presumably because of my religious background or occupation."

Now, for the first time...

You can find Janelle Taylor, Shannon Drake, Rosanne Bittner, Sylvie Sommerfield, Penelope Neri, Phoebe Conn, Bobbi Smith, and the rest of today's most popular, bestselling authors

...All in one brand-new club!

Introducing KENSINGTON CHOICE, the new Zebra/Pinnacle service that delivers the best new historical romances direct to your home, at a significant discount off the publisher's prices.

As your introduction, we invite you to accept 4 FREE BOOKS worth up to $23.96

details inside...

We've got your authors!

If you seek out the latest historical romances by today's bestselling authors, our new reader's service, KENSINGTON CHOICE, is the club for you.

KENSINGTON CHOICE is the only club where you can find authors like Janelle Taylor, Shannon Drake, Rosanne Bittner, Sylvie Sommerfield, Penelope Neri and Phoebe Conn all in one place...

...and the only service that will deliver their romances direct to your home as soon as they are published—even before they reach the bookstores.

KENSINGTON CHOICE is also the only service that will give you a substantial guaranteed discount off the publisher's prices on every one of those romances.

That's right: Every month, the Editors at Zebra and Pinnacle select four of the newest novels by our bestselling authors and rush them straight to you, even *before they reach the bookstores.* The publisher's prices for these romances range from $4.99 to $5.99—but they are always yours for the guaranteed low price of just *$3.95!*

That means you'll always save over $1.00...often as much as *$2.00*...off the publisher's prices on every new novel you get from KENSINGTON CHOICE!

All books are sent on a 10-day free examination basis, and there is no minimum number of books to buy. (A postage and handling charge of $1.50 is added to each shipment.)

As your introduction to the convenience and value of this new service, we invite you to accept

4 BOOKS FREE

The 4 books, worth up to $23.96, are our welcoming gift. You pay only $1 to help cover postage and handling.

To start your subscription to KENSINGTON CHOICE and receive your introductory package of 4 FREE romances, detach and mail the postpaid card at right *today*.

We have 4 FREE BOOKS for you as your introduction to KENSINGTON CHOICE
To get your FREE BOOKS, worth up to $23.96, mail card below.

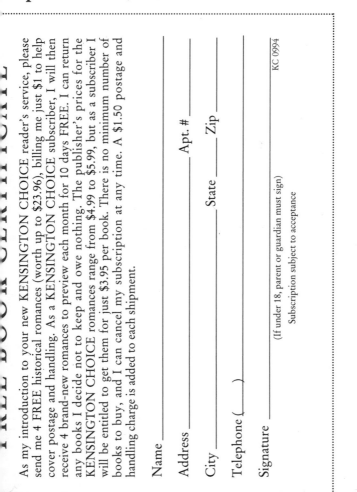

FREE BOOK CERTIFICATE

As my introduction to your new KENSINGTON CHOICE reader's service, please send me 4 FREE historical romances (worth up to $23.96), billing me just $1 to help cover postage and handling. As a KENSINGTON CHOICE subscriber, I will then receive 4 brand-new romances to preview each month for 10 days FREE. I can return any books I decide not to keep and owe nothing. The publisher's prices for the KENSINGTON CHOICE romances range from $4.99 to $5.99, but as a subscriber I will be entitled to get them for just $3.95 per book. There is no minimum number of books to buy, and I can cancel my subscription at any time. A $1.50 postage and handling charge is added to each shipment.

Name _____

Address _____ Apt. # _____

City _____ State _____ Zip _____

Telephone (___) _____

Signature _____

(If under 18, parent or guardian must sign)

Subscription subject to acceptance

KC 0994

We have
4
FREE
Historical
Romances
for you!

Details inside!

KENSINGTON CHOICE
Reader's Service
120 Brighton Road
P.O.Box 5214
Clifton, NJ 07015-5214

AFFIX
STAMP
HERE

Ten

Barbra Charms a Prime Minister and a "Master of the Game"

Playboy interviewer: "What made you change your mind [about becoming First Lady of Canada]?"
Barbra: "Certain realities."

Early in 1970, Barbra made more international headlines when she was frequently seen in the company of Pierre Elliott Trudeau. Was it love? a reporter asked Barbra's mother. "Barbra has a lot of interesting friends," Diana Kind answered, flashing an inscrutable smile.

That January 28, Barbra was Trudeau's guest at a party celebrating the Manitoba Centennial in Ottawa. She arrived with three trunks of clothes, two packed with furs. Barbra even attended a session of the Canadian Parliament and caused a stir when a member of the opposition party asked Trudeau to answer a question "if the Prime Minister can take his eyes and mind off the visitors' gallery long enough." Trudeau blushed, Barbra laughed.

According to biographer Considine, she combed newspapers for photos of them together to send her mother and relatives back home.

Trudeau would go on to marry Margaret Sinclair in 1971 and after that marriage broke up he would remain a bachelor.

In 1977 *Playboy* asked Barbra about her relationship with Trudeau, specifically whether he had asked her to marry him.

"I don't want to answer that," she demurred. "But he's an extraordinary man."

"Did you ever reflect on what it would be like to be the First Lady of Canada?" the interviewer pressed.

"Oh, yeah," Barbra acknowledged. "I thought it would be fantastic. I'd have to learn how to speak French. I would do only movies made in Canada. I had it all figured out. I would campaign for him and become totally politically involved in all the causes, abortion or whatever."

"What made you change your mind?"

"Certain realities."

Barbra would never have suggested that Trudeau consider changing *his* career. She wouldn't have wanted him to. His life was too important to a whole country, to a world.

Barbra finished work on *Pussycat* that January 19, and took time out to nest and to mother Jason.

Barbra's love for collecting beautiful things was growing apace with her income. Her buying escalated. She had been shopping for a townhouse ever since being turned down by two exclusive co-ops and she needed more space for her collections.

That March 31 Barbra closed on a five-story townhouse on East 80th Street. The house had eighteen rooms and six baths, walnut panelling in the library and den, woodburning fireplaces, and a small garden. It needed a lot of work, but Barbra paid $420,000 because she fell in love with the house's Art Deco front door. At first she was full of plans for it, beginning with those walnut panelled walls. "They're ugly," she said.

"I'm going to paint over them. They should be lacquered a nice rose color." Once she took possession, however, Barbra realized she hated the idea of living in a house in New York and never moved in.

Her disenchantment with her townhouse led Barbra to one of the most interesting father figures in her life. She had been dating John Calley, president of Warner Brothers, who introduced her to his boss, the legendary Steve Ross, head of Warner Communications, at a small dinner party. As reported in Connie Bruck's *Master of the Game,* Barbra spent the evening complaining "about having just bought a new house in New York which to her horror she now discovered needed a new roof and a new heating system. She was desperate. She couldn't afford to keep it, doubted she could sell it, it was an insupportable burden, it was ruining her life."

"How much do you want for it?" Ross asked.

"Four hundred and fifty thousand," Barbra replied.

"I'll buy it," Ross said. He—or rather his company—did so and in a month or so managed to sell it at a small profit. This marked the beginning of a mutual admiration society between Barbra and Steve Ross—another of the powerful men she turned to for advice.

Like a loyal daughter, Barbra publicly defended Ross from takeover threats mounted separately by Rupert Murdoch and Herb Siegal. The flamboyantly generous Ross and the hungry collector Barbra were the ultimate father-daughter relationship. Ross was a man who loved to give and seemingly asked nothing in return. Or almost nothing. A friend of Streisand's reported to Connie Bruck: "At Barbra's, paintings, statues—costing maybe $50,000, $100,000—were always arriving. Then the call would come—Steve would say, talk to this reporter. With Rupert Murdoch, though, she got nervous, because he owned all those newspapers. But I know at least two or three different times, Steve asked her to, and she did."

Bruck asked whether the process did not offend Barbra. The friend replied: "So what if it was obvious? She didn't care—she's a talker. She loved it."

Under Ross's tutelage, Barbra also became a tough negotiator. Ralph Peterson, Warner Bros. treasurer, told Bruck: "Barbra is very difficult. We'd make a deal with her lawyer and then she'd call and say, 'I've fired him, there's no deal.' I'd say, 'But we made a deal.' She'd say 'He agreed, I didn't. I'm sending a new lawyer.' And I'd say, 'Will he be speaking for you?' She'd say, 'Maybe yes, maybe no.' "

ACADEMY AWARDS

That February, *Dolly* had been nominated for five Academy Awards, including Best Picture, but Barbra's work was ignored. "She acted like she was very upset," a publicist told Considine, "which was ridiculous. The movie by then had clearly bombed out and the album was selling for ninety-nine cents in record stores." Nevertheless, she honored tradition and on April 7 she showed up to present the Best Actor Oscar to John Wayne for *True Grit*. Backstage in the press room, photographers begged for a shot of Barbra kissing the Duke, but she was demure: "He should kiss me," she said. He obliged, taking her in his arms and delivering a kiss on the cheek. "The big ox almost broke my ribs," she complained as she left.

That spring, Elliott's career continued to rocket forward. He had been nominated for an Academy Award for Best Actor in a Supporting Role for his work in *Bob & Carol & Ted & Alice* (the Oscar went to Gig Young for *They Shoot Horses, Don't They?*).

That April he was on the cover of *Time* magazine. The story inside described an analytical, verbal, sports-crazy, hung-up, talented, and irreverent man on his fifth movie in twelve months (and his fifth year of psychoanalysis), who was suddenly the hottest property in Hollywood. Barbra was thrilled for him.

Mel Stuart, who was directing Elliott in *I Love My Wife* told *Time*'s reporter that "Elliott is to Americans what Mastroianni is to Italians and Belmondo to the French."

Another friend said: "Barbra was not the super-humanly sensitive person she had to be in that situation, so how could they have a relationship? But they are both crazy about Jason, so something good came of it."

In November, Elliott followed the success of *M*A*S*H* and *Bob & Carol* with the release of the even more controversial *Getting Straight* which he called "a wonderful attempt at a personal statement—using a flawed, contemporary hero. The core of the film is that man's desperate struggle for some sort of identity." Barbra thought he was terrific. "I know the film upset her," Elliott told *Playboy*, "but she was moved by it. She's very critical and bright, and when it comes to acting, she's got a great eye." He was pleased by her reaction, "but it must be somewhat shocking to her to see me do things on screen that she perhaps didn't know existed."

Elliott still had fond memories of his marriage to Barbra, although he told Lewis: "I must admit that the happiest memories I have of Barbra are when we were living together before we were married. We were very dependent on each other then. We lived together because we wanted to live together, not for any legal reasons."

That June, Elliott was looking forward to the release of his production company's first film, *Little Murders*. Although the play had only a short run on Broadway, his hopes were high for the movie. "*Little Murders* is going to be a classic document," he said. "It was never meant to be a play, it was meant to be pictures."

ACTIVIST BARBRA

On June 8 Barbra threw a fund raiser for Bella Abzug in her new townhouse (Steve Ross had not yet taken it off her hands.) The outspoken Abzug was running for Congress and they had only recently met. "She came up to me," Bella reported, "and said she had a young son and wanted to do something for peace." Barbra campaigned actively for Abzug, even riding in a Greenwich Village parade. " 'You better win,' she used to tell me," Abzug says. "She was great, and I really feel indebted to her."

Barbra personally mailed three thousand invitations promising, "There will be stars of stage, screen and radio!—drinks—canapes, but *no* furniture!!"

ON A CLEAR DAY

That June, *On a Clear Day* was released, another commercial disappointment, although Barbra drew some of her finest reviews to date. Yves Montand did not emerge a fan, however. "Streisand had the right to cut this film herself," he complained, "so she cut me out so there could be more of her. Now I just have a supporting role in that film."

But Montand gave Barbra a bad rap. Paramount, already stuck with two multi-million dollar musical turkeys, *Paint Your Wagon* and *Darling-Lili,* hastily re-edited *Clear Day,* cutting it from three hours down to two and immediately going into wide release. "What the public saw was not the picture we envisioned," said a disappointed Barbra, "and I learned a very important lesson about final control." Columbia Records was so unenthusiastic that it did not release the *Clear Day* soundtrack album until a month after the film was released, and never put out a single. Convinced that the big-budget musicals were dead, Columbia would also begin to step up the pressure on Barbra to record more contemporary, i.e. rock, material.

PUSSYCAT

On November 10, *The Owl and the Pussycat* was released nationally, with a soundtrack by Blood, Sweat & Tears. Everyone agreed that Barbra was a sensation in her first non-musical film as the raucous, wise-cracking hooker with dreams. George Segal was wonderful as the book clerk with delusions of literary grandeur—the match worked. It would become one of 1971's most successful films.

BACK IN LAS VEGAS

Barbra's next step was a return to Las Vegas for back-to-back engagements at the Riviera and the Hilton International. From November 27 through December 10 she would be at the Riviera to fulfill her 1963 contract and from December 13 through January 2 she would move on to the International to fulfill a 1969 contractual obligation. Celebrities from Pearl Bailey to Franco Zeffirelli turned up to see Barbra at the Riviera. Anxious not to repeat last year's unhappy experience, Barbra came to town with a show more in the Vegas tradition. She added an opening act, comic Pat Henry, and she was accompanied by the Eddie Kendricks Singers. The new, looser Barbra was rewarded with a standing ovation on opening night.

"The last time I was here in Las Vegas I was kinda nervous," she told her audience. "It wasn't stage fright exactly. It was a thing called *Death!* I would stand in the wings, and my whole life would pass right before my eyes, but I want to tell you I've overcome this problem—now I feel absolutely great. I'm not nervous at all now. I can't breathe—but I'm not nervous." All the time she chatted, she poured tea from a pot into a china cup.

Barbra went on chatting as she produced a cigarette case, lit a fake "joint," and passed it to someone in the audience. "No, I'm not nervous at all, but I'll tell you who's nervous— the owner of this hotel is getting awfully nervous."

For Barbra it was a funny routine with a serious point—you shouldn't rely on emotional crutches. She later told *Rolling Stone:* "It was almost a sermon—no crutches, people, crutches are a no-no. First faking it. Then I started lighting live joints, passing them around to the band, you know. It was great—it relieved all my tensions. And I ended up with the greatest supply of grass ever."

According to Barbra, other acts up the Strip heard about what she was doing and "started sending me the best dope in the world. I never ran out. Hmm . . . I wonder if I should tell that story."

The year before, Barbra had tried to bring a theatrical performance to Vegas. This time she was just singing. But she bored easily and disliked singing the same songs. "I can't stand singing 'People' anymore," she confessed. "How can I impart any feeling? I really have to work hard at that—not looking bored."

Closing night at the Riviera, Nevada Governor Paul Laxalt invited Barbra to dinner, but she had to decline because she was giving a party for the crew in her dressing room. Elliott, almost unrecognizable in a heavy beard, attended her last show and visited her backstage.

Three days after closing at the Riviera, Barbra opened at the Hilton International, another triumph. It was quite an achievement for a woman who admitted to *Rolling Stone:* "I don't like to perform. That's true. I don't even like to be watched."

That December, too, she finally had another hit single,

"Stoney End." Some complained that all she'd done was cover Laura Nyro, who originally wrote and recorded the song. It was her first successful effort at a rock sound, and her first hit single in six years.

Eleven

Teaming Up With Ryan O'Neal

"If I had to marry, I mean if I was up against the wall with a rifle at my back, Babs is the girl I'd have wanted to marry."

—Ryan O'Neal

Early in 1971 rumors began to fly that a most unlikely couple had been seen around Hollywood: Barbra Streisand and Ryan O'Neal. Golden boy Ryan, whose many lovers have included Joan Collins, Farrah Fawcett, and Diana Ross, seemed like the last man to get involved with the sophisticated, quirky Barbra who was herself coming off a serious romance with the Canadian head of state.

There were those who viewed the rumored relationship with skepticism. Many were convinced that Ryan, who had just scored an enormous success as the preppy hero of *Love Story*, could only be in it for the publicity. While the affair was still just a rumor, gossip columnist Liz Smith challenged the idea that it was just a publicity stunt. "Barbra has always been appealing to men," she wrote in her syndicated column. "And why not? She has the most beautiful arms and breasts and shoulders. She's really quite a girl. I'm sure she has a

warm, realistic sex life, as she very well should have. She
obviously likes guys, and they find her to be a very juicy
person."

Barbra and Ryan had good reason to avoid being photographed together. Ryan's wife, Leigh Taylor-Young, mother
of his son Patrick, was out of the country, and a romantic
scandal, especially with someone as controversial as Barbra,
might spoil his chances for an Oscar nomination for his
work in *Love Story,* which was expected to become a 1971
box office hit. And Barbra, who remained a nice, traditional,
Jewish girl at heart, was still legally married to Elliott
Gould.

But the facts could not be denied. Ryan and Barbra were
deluding themselves if they thought that they could escape
attention when they turned up together for James Taylor's
opening at the Troubadour and at a party at the home of their
agent, Sue Mengers. They were stalked by paparazzi con-
stantly, but managed to avoid being photographed together until the March night they attended a party at the Malibu home
of record executive Robert Krasnow and later moved on to
Mama Cass Elliott's concert at Santa Monica Civic Auditorium.

Photographer Peter Borsari tried to get a picture of them
as they left the concert. Borsari claimed that he was then attacked by Ryan's younger brother, Kevin O'Neal, who threatened to smash his camera.

Ryan even brought Barbra to the Reseda ranch of his first
wife, actress Joanna Moore, where Barbra met his children,
Griffin and Tatum. At one point, they reportedly ordered his
and her gold dog tags from Cartier.

"We both fall in love easily. You wouldn't think so, would
you? I've had one marriage that didn't work; he's had two.
No one's in a rush," Barbra said.

Later, Ryan would say: "We were able to share, a kind of shyness."

ELLIOTT'S DEBACLE

While Barbra continued to soar, Elliott's own career and private life were heading for a date with disaster. After *M*A*S*H*, Elliott became the first American actor ever hired by the Swedish filmmaker Ingmar Bergman. He went to Sweden to film *The Touch*, the first English-language film by Bergman. It proved to be a mystical and life-changing experience for Elliott.

Returning to the United States, Elliott was devastated by the film's uniformly negative reviews and poor commercial performance. Critics found him miscast as a moody, mean-tempered archaeologist who becomes involved with the married Bibi Andersson, but Elliott was convinced that he had made a quantum leap as an artist. He eagerly plunged into his next film, *A Glimpse of Tiger*, with tragic consequences.

Elliott was co-producing *Tiger*, with his partner Jack Brodsky. He had met Brodsky, a publicist, while Barbra was filming *Funny Girl* in 1967, and when he and Brodsky formed their own production company and released *Little Murders* in 1971, they were among the hottest new companies in Hollywood. *A Glimpse of Tiger* was to be the first of the two-picture deal they had just signed with Warner Bros.

But he was driving himself too hard, with scarcely days between finishing one picture and starting another. He seemed driven to prove that he could be as big—or even bigger—than Barbra.

Even before shooting began on February 26, and while *Tiger* was still in rehearsal, ugly rumors flew around the production. The day filming was scheduled to begin in New York, a freak subway accident shook up the extras and crew. Although no serious injuries were reported, it was regarded as a bad omen. Next came rumors that Elliott's on-the-set temper tantrums had his co-star, Kim Darby, terrified, and that he had traded punches with director Anthony Harvey.

Unlike Barbra, who was always able to leave her work at the studio, Elliott seemed to literally *become* his character. In an interview years later, he admitted that he "frightened people on *Tiger,* but only because of my character. I showed up with a six-day beard, a cigar butt in my mouth, and a knee-length peacoat on. Around my waist, I wore an American-flag scarf. I was a wild character, and I finally couldn't—or wouldn't—vacillate between the role of actor and producer. In a sense, I scuttled my own ship."

Barbra was in California and in the middle of her romance with Ryan O'Neal, but she did what she could to mediate the dispute when Jack Brodsky turned to her for help. "Barbra was getting all this news on the phone in Los Angeles," said Ryan. "She spoke to Elliott for thirty minutes and got him to apologize. Then Brodsky would call back ten minutes later with some new item."

"Someday the world will know how bad the situation was," said director Harvey. "But Barbra was very loyal. She tried very hard to talk some sense into him."

After a hectic week of shooting, Warner shut down the film. In its story about the debacle, *Variety,* citing sources close to the production, reported that the "main problem is not so much a clash between Gould and Harvey, but that Gould himself is physically and emotionally exhausted."

"I was dying to do that picture," Elliott said later. "It just fell apart. I was very disappointed. I read a lot of bull about my being exhausted. All I can say is the best defense is always a good offense."

But he also believed that he had been "sabotaged by people

on my own payroll—cosmic embezzlers—who took and took and took and never gave back."

Elliott has always denied that drugs played any part in his career's nearly fatal turn. "I was very unstable," he admits, "but it wasn't drugs. Sure, I smoked grass and did psychedelics a little, but I was *not* a druggy or crazy."

In a compromise with Warner, he agreed to cancel the production and to pay production costs. Four years later, he said that "I owe Warner so much that in my mind they are an eternal urinal that I keep pouring my money into."

Elliott was bitter about his career-derailing encounter with Warner: "I'm a gentle soul, and in the past I had always deferred to authority. But, this time, I knew I was right, and I had to put myself to the test. The price I paid was a lot of badmouthing and no jobs for two years."

With the shutdown of *Tiger,* he was a complete emotional and physical wreck. "I'm so exhausted that I don't feel as if I can ever face another camera again," he told *Photoplay,* "but I know I shall. I have to. What else can I do with my life?"

In the aftermath, Barbra and Elliott took steps to formally end their marriage. Although Ryan had attended the Academy Awards with his wife, he lost the Oscar to George C. Scott for *Patton.* Since then, he and Barbra had been spotted more frequently in public, for example at the June 18 premiere of his new movie, *The Wild Rovers,* and he even dropped in on a recording session for her next album. Elliott had found someone new, and now it was time for Barbra to go public with her own new lover.

That June 30, Barbra and Elliott filed for divorce in a joint petition in Santo Domingo. Always eager to experiment, they became the first couple to dissolve their marriage under the Dominican Republic's new quickie divorce law. Under the statute, foreign couples and Dominicans living abroad could be divorced in less than 12 days.

Elliott had flown there and stayed only six hours in order to file the action. Barbra was represented by a local attorney.

Elliott showed up in court there with his pregnant fiancée, nineteen–year-old Jennifer Bogart. They announced that they had no plans to marry. "She'll have my children," he said, "but she won't get married. She thinks it's more romantic this way."

Their daughter Molly was born the following November. Their son, Sam, arrived in January 1973, and that December they finally married.

Although he had moved on to a new lover and started a new family, Elliott had only good words for his former wife. He was especially pleased about something Barbra had recently said about him. "She said we would always be part of each other. She really is a remarkable person."

She still mystified him. "You know something? She doesn't even listen to the radio! She doesn't know what's going on in the world—she doesn't know who Al Green is, and she's never heard the Temptations sing, and I just know she's going to love my saying that about her."

THE WILD, WONDERFUL STORY OF *WHAT'S UP, DOC?*

In a plot twist worthy of a movie of its own, *A Glimpse of Tiger,* the picture that dealt a near-fatal blow to Elliott Gould's career, would now be revamped and recast and become one of his ex-wife's greatest hits.

It began when Warner's head of production, John Calley, announced that *Tiger,* which had been in limbo since Elliott was fired, would now be converted into a vehicle for Barbra. Next, Calley approached Peter Bogdanovich about directing it. Both Calley and Barbra had seen and admired a rough cut of Bogdanovich's as-yet-unreleased film, *The Last Picture*

Show. The buzz in Hollywood was that the movie would establish Bogdanovich in the pantheon of great directors.

One problem arose immediately: Bogdanovich read the script and hated it. He dismissed *Tiger* as a kind of comedy-drama with a lot of social overtones that he didn't like at all. He suggested something more like a madcap 1930s comedy in the tradition of *Bringing Up Baby.* He made his pitch to John Calley. He wanted to do a screwball comedy. Barbra would play a wacky girl who gets involved with a very serious musicologist who is already engaged to an equally stuffy heiress. Barbra, it turned out, had something more serious in mind. Something like *The Last Picture Show.* But she was willing to go along with a comedy if she could have Ryan as her leading man.

But Bogdanovich did not want Ryan. Fortunately for movie history, Sue Mengers, the powerful Hollywood agent who was representing Barbra, Ryan, and Bogdanovich at the time, managed to broker a deal.

Bogdanovich later claimed that he had to drag Barbra "kicking and screaming through the picture. She thought we were going to do something else, and I suppose I tricked her," he said. "She'd make trouble occasionally about things that she didn't think were funny, and I'd just laugh at her. She'd ask me what I was laughing at and I'd tell her she was cute. She wouldn't know what to say to that."

Madeline Kahn was signed to star as Ryan's fiancée. She was reluctant to take the role at first. "I was a little apprehensive about Barbra," she acknowledges. "I had heard that a lot of performers wound up on the cutting-room floor in her movies, but I figured we're both Jewish, we're both from New York, I sing and she sings—so why be scared? And Peter had control."

Kahn was even franker when she talked to critic Rex Reed. "It was a movie about three people and there's only so much you could cut out of it and still have the movie make sense. So I took a chance and it turned out fine." Kahn really liked Barbra and they had some good talks. She thought they could have been friends, but Barbra had so many pressures, and was unavailable a lot on the set, so they never became close. "I got a glimpse of what it's like to be a really big superstar," said Kahn. "I don't think I'd like that."

And thus it was that a completely revamped version of *A Glimpse of Tiger* became one of Barbra's greatest hits. Did Elliott mind that his former wife starred so successfully in a role originally intended for him? Not at all. "That makes good sense to me," he said. "At least *she* made some money out of it."

That August 16, the cast and crew of *What's Up, Doc?* moved to San Francisco for location filming. Barbra and Ryan shared a suite at the Huntington Hotel and for them it was a romantic time. She had never looked better, sleek, slim, and blonde. Mengers called Barbra and Ryan "my two golden bubbies." It was also in San Francisco that Ryan suffered a serious on-set injury. He tripped over Barbra's heavy ermine coat during filming. At first, it looked like a pulled muscle. Only later would the injury be diagnosed as much more serious. Neither Barbra nor anyone else connected with *Doc* had any idea that Ryan was in tremendous pain throughout the rest of the filming.

At the end of the month, the *Doc* company relocated to the Warner Bros. lot in Burbank. There Barbra's star treatment included a trailer so lavish it embarrassed her. "Isn't it awful? I didn't ask for it, and it makes me uncomfortable," she said, surrounded by velvet couches and a crystal chandelier. "It's not good for morale on the set." Ryan defended her: "What's she gonna do in a situation like this?" he said. "If she requests another dressing room, the studio knocks her for being hard to please. And if she doesn't, everybody here on the set figures she's strutting. She can't win."

Gallant Ryan also defended his lady on television, telling an interviewer: "Everyone knocks her for being hard to please, but if she were treated like the movie queen she is, then she wouldn't have room to complain and she could feel more at ease." Barbra returned the favor, saying: "Ryan was probably the easiest actor I've ever had to work with, and the most fun. Just terrific."

Bogdanovich also defended Barbra: "I don't think there was ever a Barbra the Terrible," he insisted. "Barbra is difficult only in a delightful way. After all, she's a woman. I only wish there were more women like her in the industry."

What's Up, Doc? wrapped in October. When Barbra viewed a rough cut with Sue Mengers and John Calley, they were delighted, but she was not amused. "I know from funny," she said, "and this is *not* funny." Her expectations were so grim that she sold her gross points back to Warners Bros. for $2.5 million. She even resisted the idea of a soundtrack album, although she agreed to duet with Ryan, singing Cole Porter's "You're the Top" over the opening credits. (She also sings "As Time Goes By" in the film.) And before the movie premiered, the original bittersweet ending was changed. Barbra and Ryan were called back for additional filming in December so that their characters instead of parting at the airport, could declare their love on board the plane.

Real life ran a slightly different course, however. "By the time filming ended, Barbra and Ryan were no longer dating—and Barbra and director Peter Bogdanovich were," reported James Spada.

Director and leading lady gave one interview with Barbra in Bogdanovich's lap, feeding him pumpkin ice cream, while describing him as "a horny bastard, but brilliant." She also called him "an opinionated and autocratic director. He knows how he wants to do things and doesn't waste a lot of time. Even if he's wrong, it's the right way to do it. I gave up script approval, costume approval, everything to him."

But privately the decision to give up so much control left Barbra deeply angry. "That was a technical mistake," she would reveal later: "All through the movie I was just trying not to show my hostility toward the material. It was trying to be like *Bringing Up Baby,* but it wasn't. That was a brilliant film." She declared "I detested *Doc* . . . I didn't grow . . . It did nothing for me," she said in a press conference for UTS. She elaborated on her feelings for Joseph Gelmis of *Newsday:* "I hated it with a passion. What interests me is how many people liked it. I was embarrassed to do that film. I thought it was infantile humor and not one-sixteenth of the film it was trying to emulate."

For Barbra, good enough was just never good enough.

Although the romance with Ryan was over, Barbra was naturally concerned when he entered St. John's Hospital for back surgery that December. What had first appeared to be a sprained muscle when he fell over Barbra's ermine coat in San Francisco, turned out to be a slipped disc. Barbra marveled that, "I never heard him complain. I never dreamed he was hurt that badly."

Now he lay in the hospital and there was nothing she could do for him. "The terrible irony is that you're with somebody so much and just when you need to be with him, you can't be," she said. They did stay in touch by phone, and she flew back to Los Angeles twice to visit him in the hospital. "Ryan was lying in bed, and you know, he has that terribly irresistible little boy quality about him. I have that Brooklyn Jewish need to mother. Maybe that's why we got along so well."

But Barbra had a commitment to appear in Las Vegas for the 1972–1973 holidays, while Ryan's wife was free to visit him daily.

Barbra insists that to her, Ryan was always more than a

pretty face. "I don't think externals are so important as many people think. I feel secure with men of all kinds, whatever they look like, but I think most women hesitate to pair up, permanently, with a man who's . . . outrageously handsome. Anyway, what's inside is what tells. I never cared for dumb dons; I want a man with brains upstairs, you know?"

Years later, Ryan was asked why he and Barbra had not married. His reply: "Well, that's very personal, and there are many reasons, but I occasionally think about it and I'll just say this about that—If I had to marry, I mean if I was up against the wall with a rifle at my back, Babs is the girl I'd have wanted to marry."

NEW DIRECTIONS IN RECORDINGS

With guidance from Clive Davis, Barbra was attempting a new direction in her recording work. He teamed her with record producer Richard Perry, and encouraged her to record material by up-and-coming songwriters her own age. Her next album, *Stoney End,* took its title from her hit single. She also included "I Don't Know Where I Stand," by Joni Mitchell, Randy Newman's "I'll be Home," and Harry Nilsson's "Maybe." The *Stoney End* album, released in February, would go platinum before the end of the year.

Most music critics praised Barbra's first tentative steps in a new direction. Stephen Holden of the *New York Times* later wrote that "Most of [*Stoney End's*] songs came out of the hip Brill Building school of pop-rock which Miss Streisand had until then completely ignored. The three Laura Nyro songs at the album's center combined primitive and urbane ingredients that accommodated Miss Streisand's emotionality, while they encouraged her to relax her phrasing more than she had ever done."

Marty Erlichman was the one who promoted the "Stoney

End" single into a hit, but sometimes his single-minded devotion to his client went too far. According to Clive Davis, this led to one of the major disasters of the *Stoney End* publicity effort.

"The *Stoney End* album's advertising campaign was aimed, logically enough, at young audiences. We spent nearly a hundred thousand dollars advertising it in underground papers, rock magazines, *Rolling Stone,* and on all the major FM stations. 'Barbra is as young as the writers on this album,' we said, and we listed their names in large, bold type. Fine—except that it convinced Erlichman and Streisand to go all the way and try to capture the *Rolling Stone* crowd as well. She agreed to an interview which led to a story titled 'The Jeaning of Barbra Streisand.'

"*Rolling Stone* has made a tremendous contribution to contemporary music," said Davis, "but it also consistently takes a snide attitude toward 'establishment' artists: a lack of purity is assumed, I suppose. This story was no exception; Barbra was pictured as an old-style movie-star type living in the glittering Hollywood Hills and incongruously wearing dungarees. It didn't match, and the magazine hammered this home."

Perry would also produce her next album, *Barbra Joan Streisand,* which included John Lennon's "Mother" which Stephen Holden, writing in *Rolling Stone,* called "an unqualified bummer" and a more Barbra-esque Burt Bachrach-Hal David medley which Holden called "The high point of the album . . . pure vintage Streisand." The more mainstream Morgan Ames of *High Fidelity* said that "To say this is a 'new Streisand' implies that she has shed an old self. Yes and no—mostly no. What this album displays is an alive and growing Streisand." Released that August, it would become Barbra's eleventh million-selling album by the end of the year.

BARBRA BACK TO VEGAS

Barbra returned to Las Vegas reluctantly that November because she had to fulfill her long-standing commitment to the Hilton. Comedian Robert Klein opened for her and experienced the same thing she had on her first visit to the town: the audience didn't quite get his material. Barbra herself was slightly more comfortable this time around. Critics found her warmer and more relaxed. She still eschewed Strip-style glamour and instead of glitzy evening gowns, she appeared in black leather or white silk pantsuits, looking slim and gorgeous. She even bantered freely with the audience. One night, when a fan yelled out "Barbra, let your hair down!" she shot back: "After it took me an hour to get it up?"

She brought along the now-familiar stool and tea table, props that helped her get through her last Vegas stint, and she poked fun at her last appearance with pot jokes and references to Liberace. She referred to her small club days nostalgically. As the lights dimmed and left Barbra in a spotlight, she felt like she was back at the Bon Soir again and it was a nice feeling. "As she sings, she is confident enough to reach out for her audience, but not so overconfident that she takes it for granted," wrote critic Robert Hilburn of the *Los Angeles Times*. "It's a very natural performance, almost as if she were singing for friends in her living room. She always had the voice, now she has the manner as well."

Twelve

Barbra's Flop: Up the Sandbox

"When a nice Jewish girl from Brooklyn can play a WASP who fantasizes, you know you've got an actress."
—Marty Erlichman

Barbra welcomed the new year 1972 at the Hilton International and by the time she closed out her engagement there on January 13 she had proven that she could master even that tough town. The following day she was the subject of an Ed Sullivan special, "Entertainer of the Year," originating live from Caesar's Palace. Technically, Barbra still had eight years to run on her contract with the Hilton, but it would be more than two decades before she returned to Vegas.

She threw herself into preparations for her next film, *Up the Sandbox,* which would be the first of three planned for her new production company, First Artists. Based on the novel by Anne Richardson Roiphe, *Up the Sandbox* was the story of an unhappy young Manhattan housewife, Margaret Reynolds, who discovers she is pregnant with a third child at the same time that she is questioning her life, her marriage, and the position of women in general. She fantasizes about confronting the woman she suspects is her husband's mistress, blowing up a Manhattan monument, and even meeting Fidel Castro, who reveals to her that he is really a woman in drag.

Barbra was not crazy about going to work again. Through her friends, the lyricists Alan and Marilyn Bergman, she had discovered tennis and typically was immersing herself in the game. In spite of all the work she put into it, she would remain a scrappy but merely ordinary player.

Between tennis sets she read and liked Roiphe's novel and the opportunity the screenplay offered to play so many different roles in Margaret's fantasies. For the first film project that she would control she chose her personnel carefully. She wanted to be surrounded by excellence and by people she trusted. Marty Erlichman would be her associate producer and longtime friend Cis Corman her casting director.

For her director, Barbra chose Irvin Kershner. They had met and become friends after he wrote her a note praising her work in *Funny Girl*. Yet he was not awed about working with her. At the start of rehearsals Kershner told Barbra: "I've heard things about you—that you're tough, that you can be killer." Kershner told her what exactly he had heard and what his fears were. "And she laughed, and said, 'Well, I don't think I'm those things. I have nothing to say . . . I don't know what to say.' " But Kershner felt he had cleared the air.

"She is not difficult to work with, but she is wary of amateurs," he told Streisand biographer Shaun Considine. "She detests mediocrity. She's been screwed so many times by bad judgment that she feels until she can trust you, she'll make her own decisions. Watch her work, you'll be surprised."

This love fest between Kershner and Barbra set the tone for the entire film. "I never found her bitchy," said Kershner. "I never found her competitive. I find that she fights to maintain her artistic integrity, right or wrong. This is what she feels has to be done and she'll fight for it. But she's not a vicious person in any way. It was impossible for her to ever fire anyone who was really doing something terrible to her. She couldn't do it." Barbra even threw Friday night parties for the crew and served them cookies she baked herself.

According to Kershner, "We never really had an argument. That doesn't mean we didn't have *conflict*—but it wasn't personal conflict."

David Selby, who played her husband, was a relative unknown. "I had the break of working with Barbra Streisand," he acknowledged later, "and the misfortune to be her husband—the villain of the piece—in her least popular film. I wouldn't have traded the experience. We were both at our peak, and she was very maternal, with kids all around her. Funny, it was a feminist film, but she was very soft and vulnerable, and from what I heard, less concerned with appearances and talking things out. It was hard work, but not strained. We thought it would be a breakthrough film, but no one was satisfied with it: not feminists, not anti-feminists, not the fans, nor the people who'd read the book. Oh, well. Now it's nostalgia."

BARBRA IN AFRICA

Sandbox was filmed in New York and Los Angeles, but some of the most memorable scenes were shot on location in East Africa that May. Barbra's pregnant character goes on safari to find the primitive tribe that is rumored to have discovered painless childbirth. The scenes were filmed among the Sambura tribe about 200 miles north of Nairobi.

Barbra brought Jason along for the experience. "I mean all my life I've been scared to death of animals. I'm a person whose whole life has been full of fear. You know, the whole Jewish mother syndrome. I mean, I was scared to look at animals in the zoo. But here it all seemed so natural. Although if I never see another wild animal again, I think I can survive.

But it was all so natural, and I felt part of it. I know that Jason is not going to be afraid the way I was. It is all worth it for that."

Barbra actually got to like proximity to the jungle. "I was afraid to come here. I'm afraid of wild animals," she acknowledged. "I'm not a zoo person. After a while here, though, you are less frightened, then you are blase, then you realize how beautiful it is. You walk to work in the morning and see a giraffe, and realize that it's his land."

It was Barbra's first exposure to such a radically different culture and she approached it with an open mind. "At first, we were suspicious of them and they were suspicious of us," she admitted. "There were animal droppings all around. The people have dirt on their hands, maybe from the time they were born. They don't have any soap. I gave some women a few Wash 'n Dri's. But, you know, they probably didn't like it."

The life was incredibly simple compared to life at home. "They own nothing—except themselves," she marveled. But the sexual mores left something to be desired. "These women are not permitted to experience pleasure, nor are they permitted to show pain. They can't even scream when they have a baby. They seem happy but wow! Who am I to say anything, to preach?"

After location filming in Africa ended in June, Barbra, Kershner, and Jason took time out for some sightseeing in Israel. It was Barbra's first visit. But illness forced her to cancel a visit with Premier Golda Meir and return to California.

"WRITE SOMETHING FOR BARBRA"

While Barbra was completing *Up the Sandbox,* her old nemesis Ray Stark was looking for the next vehicle under her contract with him.

Stark reportedly asked Arthur Laurents, director of *I Can*

Get for You Wholesale, to "write something for Barbra." Laurents came up with a fifty-page treatment that Barbra just loved. There were at least five great scenes in it and she knew that they would carry the film. The role that Laurents had created for her was Katie Morosky, a passionate young Jewish woman of the 1930s, a political activist and committed liberal. She was a character Barbra immediately identified with.

The story itself was a classic American romance in the tradition of *Love Story.* Katie Morosky is an ugly duckling working her way through Cornell University during the Great Depression and majoring in leftist causes. During World War II she marries her old classmate, handsome blond WASP Hubbell Gardiner and later tries in vain to change her own nature to fit into the life he wants.

That April it was announced that Barbra's next film for Rastar would be *The Way We Were.* Now all Barbra needed was a director and a leading man. She wanted Ryan O'Neal, but Stark felt she had already teamed with him once and he wanted to see her with someone new for some fresh chemistry. Next, she targeted Warren Beatty. Like Ryan, Beatty was known for romancing some of the most beautiful stars in town, including Julie Christie and Joan Collins. Warren and Barbra also shared a profound commitment to the ideals of the Democratic party and at that time Warren was closely involved in Senator George McGovern's presidential campaign. With his good looks and his political ideals, he seemed perfect for the role of Hubbell Gardiner.

A "FLING" WITH WARREN BEATTY

Warren indicated he was interested in co-starring with Barbra in *The Way We Were* and Barbra's agent, Sue Mengers, arranged a meeting for them to discuss their mutual interests. But Warren was far more interested in Barbra's drawing power for a political benefit he was planning than in sharing the screen with her.

"Both Warren and Barbra, when they wanted something, could be very seductive," an insider told Considine. "So the games went on and soon they were in bed. It went on for weeks. They'd meet at her house, or at El Escondido, his hide-away suite at the Beverly Wilshire. Warren was relentless. He worked on her head. And on her hands, feet, and shoulders. Barbra matched him, stroke for stroke. He'd get her into bed and he'd turn on the famous Beatty charm, and then he'd slip in a plug for the concert. He'd whisper, 'Barbra, you *should* do it. You *have* to do it. It's your civic duty. For me, baby, come on, come on.' And Barbra would moan and sigh and say, 'Oh, I know, Warren. I know. I *am* considering it. Now let's read some more of the script.' And he'd say, 'Okay, Barbra. You want to take it from the top or the bottom this time?'"

Barbra eventually yielded to Warren's urging and agreed to shelve her fears about performing in public to join three other music stars, Carole King, James Taylor, and Quincy Jones, in a live concert at the Hollywood Forum. The "Four for McGovern" concert was designed to raise money for Senator McGovern's presidential campaign.

It would be Barbra's first live concert appearance in five years. "When you have a nerd like Nixon in the White House, we performers—not just as artists but as *individuals*—have to do something. We're still in Vietnam; we've still got our sticky fingers all over the whole planet, and it's time we stopped somewhere," she said as she announced her commitment to the event.

The "Four for McGovern" concert on April 15 drew 18,000 people. At the time, James Taylor was well known for two hits: his own "Fire and Rain," and his cover of King's "You've got a Friend." King's album *Tapestry* was on its way to becoming the bestselling album of all time. Lou Adler, King's producer who was also producing the event, wanted her to close the show.

But, as usual when Barbra performed, Marty Erlichman was by her side and tireless in protecting his star's interests. Clive Davis recalls, "Streisand was a 'closing' artist—a superstar who *always* closes the show—and Erlichman felt that it might be a slap in her face." Finally it was agreed—Barbra would close the show.

But the real question remained: Would Barbra appear at all? Although philosophically committed to the concert, she was terrified of performing, especially in front of a predominantly youthful audience that, she was convinced, was really there to see Carole King and James Taylor. Beatty kept assuring her that the crowd was there as much to see her as the other acts. In fact, it was Barbra's fans who had filled the most expensive, $100–a-ticket seats and for that the fundraisers were grateful.

James Taylor and Carole King opened with "Song of Long Ago" and "Close Your Eyes," performed individually and then together. "A delay followed because a large orchestra had to assemble to back up Barbra; the audience began to fidget," Clive Davis recalled. "But as soon as the loudspeaker announced her and she came onstage, it was clear that everything would be fine. She was greeted with a thunderous ovation."

"She began with 'Sing,' from *Sesame Street*, performed at the request of her son Jason, and soon moved into 'Make Your Own Kind of Music,' " Davis recalled. "She made some small talk, including some pot jokes that went over well with the young crowd. She moved into more ballads, but brought down the house with a rousing version of Carole King's 'Where You Lead.' When one fan yelled "We love you Barbra," she responded, "Still?" There was more to come, but she still hadn't decided on a closing and gave the audience a choice: "Stoney

End" or "Secondhand Rose," as if asking them to vote on which direction her career should take. The voice vote, like Barbra's own musical taste, was split, but with only time enough for one she chose "Stoney End." After that, she had the crowd in the palm of her hand. This was a *live* audience and she was a performer without peer. It was one of popular music's legendary concert performances and the evening belonged to her. The press and word-of-mouth comment was so phenomenal that we released a live album; it went gold immediately."

Ben Fong-Torres of *Rolling Stone* dubbed the "Four for McGovern" concert "the most glamorous pop concert in recent Hollywood history," and said that Barbra—not the late arriving George McGovern—was the real star of the evening. "Nothing—not even her own acute show-and-tells about her greenery—can dim the fact that Streisand is a star and, on this night, *the* star."

After the concert, Warren decided he wasn't interested in co-starring with Barbra in *The Way We Were* after all and resumed his relationship with his longtime companion, Julie Christie. "Julie had been out of town when Warren and Barbra were making whoopee," an insider told Considine. "She had been in England visiting her family, but once she was back in L.A. and the Forum concert was over, Warren resumed with Julie and bid *adieu* to Barbra." Barbra later dismissed her relationship with Warren Beatty as "one of my flings."

Although "Four for McGovern" raised over $300,000, by the time expenses were deducted it netted a mere $18,000. The person who profited most was probably Barbra, who came out of it with a concert album that she released the following November. And instead of Warren Beatty as her co-star for *The Way We Were* she had to settle for Robert Redford, leading to one of the greatest successes of her film career.

THE WAY IT WAS

Columbia Pictures desperately needed a hit, and was pressing Barbra and Ray Stark to begin *The Way We Were,* but the project was still a love story without a leading man. Sydney Pollack, who had been nominated for an Academy Award for Best Director of *They Shoot Horses, Don't They?*, was signed to direct. (He lost the Oscar to John Schlesinger, who had directed *Midnight Cowboy.*) Pollack immediately went after Robert Redford, whom he had directed so successfully in *Jeremiah Johnson.* But Redford, like Warren Beatty before him, recognized that Barbra had all the good scenes and he had no desire to play a subordinate role. He believed Hubbell's detached WASP cool was no match for the heat of Katie's commitment. Pollack insisted that Redford was the only actor strong enough not to be overshadowed by Barbra on screen.

"It wasn't that there weren't other actors who could act," said Pollack. "But they didn't look like Bob. You had to have a WASP—an all-American, blond, blue-eyed. Newman was too old. Ryan [O'Neal] is a good actor in certain things, but [Barbra] was just too strong."

"I had turned it down because it was overly sentimental and drippy," Redford said. "I also thought the politics in it was bullshit. It was knee-jerk liberalism and very arch. But there was some very good love-story writing, which read to me like an old-fashioned Hollywood movie."

The script was revised and revised again to make it more acceptable to Redford.

At last, pressed by Columbia, Ray Stark told Pollack he had one hour to sign Redford, then they had to move on to someone else. Redford signed.

"Finally, I just took the part on faith," he said.

Even after taking the part, however, Redford resisted Barbra's requests that they meet to discuss the production. Barbra, always more vulnerable than outsiders realized, was hurt by his distance. Did he dislike her? Sydney Pollack spoke to Redford, telling him: "You've got to see her because she's taking it personally." Redford agreed to meet with Barbra, but only if Pollack went along. So the three of them sat down to dinner at her house and talked. "We had about three meetings before the picture began—that's all," said Pollack.

Filming began that August 21, in Williamstown, Massachusetts, with Williams College standing in for Cornell. The project itself was an education in the star mentality for many involved. "You want to talk clothes and wigs here?" an unnamed production assistant confided to biographer Considine. "[Barbra] went *bananas*. She was trying on outfits and posing for test shots for weeks. For one scene she wanted to wear jeans and a custom-fitted T-shirt. She was told that women in the forties didn't wear T-shirts or blue jeans. 'But I look so cute in the outfit,' she argued. Then she picked up a line in the script where her character went to Harlem each week to have her hair straightened. Now, *that* was character development for Barbra. She drove her hair stylists *crazy*. She had them burning wigs by the mile to get the look she wanted. And her nails; that was another story. In the opening scenes she was supposed to be playing a dowdy college activist, but she wore these long red fingernails, like a Revlon model. She refused to cut them. Robert Redford wouldn't cut his hair either. *He* was playing a naval officer during World War II. They had regulation haircuts then, but not according to Bobby. He had to have that boyish, tousled look. He was a star, she was a star, so hooray for Hollywood."

Said their director Sydney Pollack: "She would see the dailies and think he was wonderful and she stunk. But they're very alike in that respect, because he would see them and think that she was wonderful and he stunk." Said Redford: "She'd talk and talk and talk and drive me nuts. And the amusing thing was that after she'd talk and talk and talk, we'd get down to doing (the scene) and she'd do just what she was going to do from the beginning."

But Barbra brought a heat to her scenes with Redford that no other actress ever has.

"Barbra . . . I can't explain it," said Redford. "Her femininity brings out the masculinity in a man, and her masculinity brings out a man's femininity, vulnerability, romanticism, whatever you want to call it. It's a crude way of putting it, but that's what it boils down to."

SANDBOX OPENS—WITH A THUD

Barbra had already wrapped *The Way We Were* when *Sandbox* opened that December. The picture was so personally important to her that she took time off to promote it at a press conference at the Beverly Wilshire.

For Barbra, one of the most important messages of the film was that "a woman doesn't have to lose her children to be a credit to the world. In the film Margaret decides that through our children miracles can happen, we can evolve to a happier people."

Barbra also repeated the press conference ordeal at the "21" club in New York. Barbra used the occasion to discuss her acting. "I told Kershner I'd like to do a film where I do nothing," she said. "When I was fifteen years old, watching acting classes, what impressed me most was the beauty of nothingness—actors just doing relaxation exercises. I learned a lesson then in letting yourself be nothing. Because nothing is something. A person can't really be nothing, know what I mean? In all my other films, I played characters full of idiosyncrasies, with lots of funny lines. In this one, I get back to my beginnings. Understand what I mean?" But as she looked around the room at the gathered reporters, she could see that they didn't, so she gave a demonstration: a limpness exercise from her acting class.

"It's a picture that has to be seen more than once to catch all the meanings and shadings. I didn't care how they filmed me or from what angles. I was being Margaret, and I didn't want her well lighted or with her hair glossy," Barbra said. "As an actor, you strive for simplicity. There are flaws in this picture. That's part of life. I don't mind them."

Marty Erlichman waxed enthusiastic after early previews. "When a nice Jewish girl from Brooklyn can play a WASP who fantasizes, you know you've got an actress," he said. "Did you know that we did not get one card at any of the previews that objected to casting Barbra as a WASP?"

But prospects for *Sandbox* were damaged even before it opened when it received an "R" rating from the Motion Picture Board. It was deemed for adults only because of the bare-breasted African women and a scene where Fidel Castro reveals himself to be a female. Barbra was outraged. "What kind of morality do you have when people would rather have children see blood and gore than a woman's breast?" she asked.

Barbra showed up at the opening December 21 escorted by screenwriter David Rafiel. But audiences expecting another madcap comedy in the style of *What's Up, Doc?*, were disappointed. Reviews were mixed, although most critics praised Barbra's performance. Even her old antagonist Rex Reed found her "loveable" and wrote that, "This refreshing, imaginative, and tenderly moving comedy provides her with her finest role to date and she rises to the challenge cunningly. . . . The maturity, the depth and the vision she has achieved as a woman and an actress are really joyous to observe." Donald J. Mayerson of *Cue* wrote: "Streisand's Walter Mitty vignettes—working with black revolutionaries to blow up the Statue of Liberty or rebelling against an officious mother—are gems of humor and insight. This is a fine film and an important one in its treatment of female vs. femininity."

Up the Sandbox might be said to be her first political film, with its discussion of abortion and women's choices. It was the first developed by her own production company. But it was also her first flop. Barbra drew fine notices for her performance as a repressed, fantasizing mother. Some called it the best performance of her career. But it was not the "Streisand" performance that ticket-buyers and her fans wanted and it was soon written off as a bomb.

Director Kershner was philosophical: "I don't think people wanted to see Barbra Streisand playing an ordinary housewife who has fantasies and babies."

Barbra continued to regard the film as some of her finest work to date. For her it had been an artistically rewarding experience and she didn't care that it failed financially. A year later she was still defending it. "I liked *Up the Sandbox*," she insisted. "That was my statement about what it means to be a woman. It's what I wanted to say, and I'm glad I said it, even if it doesn't make a nickel."

As the year ended, Barbra could at least take some cheer from the reception to her latest album, *Live Concert at the Forum,* produced by Richard Perry, and drawn mainly from tapes of the "Four for McGovern" concert. *Variety* called it "a winner all the way. Barbra Streisand is at the top of her form in an excellent choice of contemporary and standard ballads." *Movie Digest* praised her singing and material, noting: "This concert may not be so well recorded as some of Barbra's studio albums, but it benefits greatly from her superb showmanship and her empathetic rapport with an audience. A Streisand triumph."

Barbra's fundraising work did not help George McGovern, however. Richard Nixon was reelected by a landslide that November, much to her chagrin. She could not understand it.

"Maybe people are afraid of change," she said. "It's as if they've grown almost comfortable with corruption. I mean, Nixon is so *obviously* dishonest. His promise to end the war in Vietnam was just par for the course, wasn't it? I don't know, it's all so *self*-destructive. But then I believe the world is moving toward inevitable self-destruction."

Thirteen

Jon Peters, the Man Who . . .

"Maybe I liked Jon from the start because he practically told me to get lost. He was the man, I the woman—that was very clear from the beginning."

—Barbra

In 1973 Barbra would meet the man who would change her life, but the year did not start well. Barbra was involved in an affair with an Arizona real estate tycoon. She ended the relationship when she realized that he would never leave his wife. She was alone, and her latest film, *Up the Sandbox,* had opened to disappointing reviews and box offices.

At 31, Barbra had never looked better. Photographer Richard Avedon, who had photographed her for her first *Vogue* cover and was now flown to London to photograph her for a new *Vogue* story, had spent a lifetime photographing the most beautiful women in the world, and had long since fallen under her spell. "Ten years ago, she simply decided to be beautiful and now she is. It's sheer willpower."

Barbra had made important decisions about her career. "My object now is to get rid of all my professional obligations, to conclude any contracts I have, to do whatever I must to be free of commitments. With records, television, films, I've spent ten years in bondage more or less. Now I want to work only when I want to work."

Except for one session in which she recorded the theme for *Sandbox,* "If I Close My Eyes," Barbra had not been inside a recording studio in two years. That March she returned to begin work simultaneously on two albums, one classical, the other contemporary pop with music by Michel Legrand and lyrics by her good friends Alan and Marilyn Bergman. Both projects were aborted and the results never released.

In May, Barbra sang at a Beverly Hills birthday party honoring Daniel Ellsberg, the man who had leaked the Pentagon Papers to the media. The purpose of the party was to raise funds for Ellsberg's defense and for pledges of one hundred dollars to one thousand dollars, she sang requests, in person or over the phone. "If you called in and pledged such and such a sum, she'd sing it in your ear," a guest that night told Shaun Considine. "It was terrific fun. She did a duet of 'Twinkle, Twinkle, Little Star' with Carl Reiner. She also sang 'Long Ago and Far Away,' 'Someone to Watch over Me,' 'You're the Top,' and 'Happy Birthday' to Ellsberg." That night, Barbra raised close to fifty thousand dollars for Ellsberg's defense. For her pains, Barbra was named to Nixon's fabled "enemies list." She was so shocked and frightened by this that she retreated from active campaigning for the next fourteen years, while quietly continuing to donate generously to political causes she believed in.

In spite of her successes, Barbra was feeling powerless that summer. She could not get her record company to release her Ellsberg evening as an album, she was still tied to Ray Stark, and she was still committed to the CBS network for a fifth and final special on her 1967 contract.

"It wasn't that we were above doing television," Marty Erlichman insisted. "We just couldn't agree on the type of show to do, or whom she should appear with."

Erlichman had a dream: he wanted to team Barbra with her male equivalent, Frank Sinatra. Fortunately, Sinatra was a longtime admirer. The match Erlichman proposed to Sinatra's lawyer, Mickey Rudin, was beautiful in its simplicity: "I proposed that since Barbra had a commitment to a network and no sponsor, and Sinatra had a sponsor and no network, that we should have them team up. No guests—just these two— singing. We could do two shows, back to back. That way we'd own one and he'd own the other. One would be on CBS, the other of his choice. We'd split everything down the middle— two specials, two record albums. Mickey got back to me and said Frank would do one, not two. One became too much of a problem for us. Also Frank's sponsor was a beer company and that didn't seem right for Barbra. I told her, 'There are things you should have as part of your lifetime. When you get older, you can sit back and look at it and say you have played with all of the best.' There would have been nothing wrong for her to work with Sinatra. When you're as big as he is, it's part of history. But she didn't want to actively pursue it. She was more interested in going it alone. So the deal fell apart."

There were rumors that Barbra's television hiatus was because of a conflict between Marty Erlichman and the network's programming chief, Mike Dann. Barbra's contract with the network gave her complete creative control. As Erlichman put it: "If Barbra wanted to sing with a piano for an hour and pocket all the money she would have saved, she could have, and CBS could say nothing about it." But creative control was meaningless when the network did not support her. Dann had openly scorned her first special, *My Name is Barbra,* which went on to sweep the Emmies. Erlichman had pleaded with him to schedule *A Happening in Central Park* during the summer of 1968, to build pre-release publicity for *Funny Girl,* the movie, but instead the special aired on September 15, coinciding with the premiere. After that experience, Erlichman vowed never to work with Dann again. Now Dann was gone and Fred Silverman was in charge. Marty and Barbra were willing to work with the network again.

Barbra had her own reasons for not returning to television for five years. "I've been busy and—I don't like to work that hard. It takes a lot of time to do a special, and I really didn't have the time or the interest. In the time it took me to do this special, you could do a whole movie."

In the spring Barbra began taping her final CBS-TV special. Her only guest star would be Ray Charles. They rehearsed in New York and Los Angeles and recorded at the Elstree Studios in London that May.

ENTER JON PETERS

That August, Jon Peters tossed his comb and patented razor-scissors into his red Ferrari and headed for Barbra's Holmby Hills mansion. She wanted him to work on her wig for her next film, *For Pete's Sake.*

Actually, it started even before that. "I saw a woman at a party," Barbra said later, "and Jon had done her hair. It was perfect for the movie—half an inch all over the head. Meanwhile, I got a message from a friend that Jon Peters wanted to meet me."

The half-Cherokee, half-Italian native of Van Nuys, California, frankly admitted that he had wanted to make his own movies since the age of ten, when he worked as an extra in Cecil B. De Mille's *The Ten Commandments.* He had spent time in reform school and ended his formal education at thirteen. He learned the hairdressing trade from relatives, wandered the world, and was the divorced father of a son by the time he was nineteen.

Up until the time he met Barbra, Jon's claim to fame was bringing the blow-dry look to Southern California and making his first million via his chain of high-style hair salons before he was thirty.

When Jon arrived at Barbra's house for their first appointment, she kept him waiting for an hour and a half. He was ready to leave. Then Barbra came down and explained that she wanted him to do her wig. "I never do wigs. What an insult!" he fumed. He didn't like to do wigs, he didn't like to be kept waiting. He also told her she had a great ass.

Another interviewer asked Peters if he was concerned about Barbra's reaction, he answered quickly: "No, because at the time I thought *I* was the biggest star in the world and I couldn't understand how she could keep me waiting."

"Actually I met Barbra when I was ending a cycle in my life. I'd been in business for seventeen years and one of the people I'd never done was Barbra. I didn't want to quit without doing her, so I put out a call to people I'd go anywhere anytime to cut her hair."

Well, he did the wig, as well as the wigs for Barbra's next movie, *Funny Lady*. But it took a while for romance to blossom.

For one thing, Barbra resisted. He was just not her type. But she had yet to experience his greatest strength: his tenacity. They also shared an enormous drive and a difficult childhood. Both lost their fathers early in life and had stepfathers they characterized as "abusive."

"Stop coming after me," she told Peters. "You're not my type."

Barbra liked tennis, Peters had never played, but he soon showed up with a racquet and, without even knowing how to keep score, beat her. This got Barbra's attention.

"Then I told him I liked more distinguished men," she told Diane Shah of the *New York Times*. "Men who smoked pipes. So he comes over wearing a velvet jacket over a T-shirt and jeans, glasses and a pipe. He even traded his Ferrari for a Jag. Jon never lets up."

She was also impressed with his independence. "Maybe I liked Jon from the start because he practically told me to get lost," she said. He was the man and I the woman—that was very clear from the beginning." Peters explained it slightly differently: "Neither one of us dominates the other all the time. We dominate each other at different times. I feel, anyway, that to be able to make any relationship work, each person has to give 60–40."

Peters also knew how to treat a woman. He didn't get rich on hair alone. He was forever telling Barbra how good she looked. He was the first man who told her she was sexy, she had a great ass. Why didn't she show her body more in movies? "He was instrumental in a new, younger me," she told Shah. "This hipper, more sexual character. But it was very entrepreneurial. Jon just had that instinct in him."

Further, he recognized in Barbra a soulmate. "I didn't fall in love with Barbra independent of her star trip," he told *Women's Wear Daily*. "I was fascinated by her, and, of course, by Hollywood."

Soon Barbra and Jon were taking their sons Christopher Peters and Jason Gould on family outings to Disneyland, skiing together in Vail, Colorado.

"I went with Jon Peters because he knew what to do on Sundays," she said.

"I was a recluse until I met her," Jon claimed. "She's so many different people and so am I." He gave her a Palomino horse for her thirty-second birthday and began sprinkling his conversation with Yiddishisms.

Although most of Hollywood was amazed about the new

relationship, to Barbra and Jon it seemed the most natural pairing in the world.

One reason so many were hostile to Peters was his attitude. He was not intimidated by the most powerful people in the movie business. "I don't think that producing a film Is any great magic," he said. "It's just a matter of a lot of hard work and dedication and getting the best people you can. I feel lucky to be working with a person of Barbra's experience."

Peters was not someone who stroked egos. "Oh, I never held any hands in the hair business and I don't now," he boasted. "I ran my business the way I thought it should be run and I'm going to produce films the way I feel they have to be produced. I'm not too much of a coddler. I'm too truthful for that."

Barbra was intensely loyal. "So what if Jon was a hairdresser! Is that not supposed to happen? It's a very narrow way of thinking. A lot of producers started off selling dresses in New York. They said the same kind of thing about me. 'How can she act when she's just a singer?' No one is *just* anything. The whole purpose of life is to grow, right?

"Jon has done a lot to open my life. He's a very strong man. I'm basically lazy and Jon looks after the business side of things. He's exposed me to a lot of things I wasn't aware of before, like gardening and health foods. He fights for what he believes in. He doesn't let people walk all over him."

And that included Barbra herself. In the beginning it wasn't easy. "He took me to a party once and said he wanted to go for a walk with me, then put me on his shoulders and wouldn't let me down," she recalled. "He was so vital, so virile, really terrific and alive. He's half Cherokee Indian, you know, and he's not frightened by the sea or the mountains or snakes or things that I'm afraid of. And I like a man who isn't afraid."

At last she had met a man who shared her drive, her creativity, her perfectionism. Elliott had been just as shaken as Barbra when her success hit so soon, so hard, and their separate careers had driven them further apart. Her later lovers, especially Ryan O'Neal and Omar Sharif, had offered her passion but they lacked the street-smart toughness she needed to match her own. She and Jon shared a fiery ambition, and boundless passion.

Neither of them would be the same. Like Barbra, Peters was blessed with a healthy ego. In fact, he had already given interviews in which he claimed that she was one of his clients and implied that he had no use for her. Three years earlier, in 1970, he told *TV Guide:* "In the last five years I've made a lotta, lotta, lotta money. I hate actresses, though. I used to do Streisand and all the big stars and they drive me nuts! I'm not anybody's slave." In fact, at the time he told that to *TV Guide,* Jon had not even met Barbra.

The Way We Were opened late in October. Barbra herself was so pleased with the way the picture had turned out that she had agreed to sing the theme song, with music by Marvin Hamlisch and lyrics by Alan and Marilyn Bergman, over the opening and closing credits. (She may have also been prompted by the suspicion that Redford had very quietly stolen the picture from her and was looking to re-establish some balance.) The movie theme was considered too slow-paced for a single, and so Barbra recorded another version which was released as a single on September 26. It became her first chart-topping single and the biggest record of her career to date, ending up the top pop single of 1974.

As *The Way We Were* began to demonstrate signs it would be the blockbuster hit of 1973, the momentum pushed Barbra's single up the record charts. Cashing in on the movie's popularity, Columbia Records proceeded to bring out *two* albums titled *The Way We Were.* One was a straight soundtrack album, the only time Barbra was heard was singing the movie theme as she had over the opening and closing credits. The second album, truly a Streisand album, consisted mainly of previously unreleased material from earlier sessions.

Barbra did go into the studio to record some fresh songs for the album that December, and Jon joined her for some of the sessions. And then suddenly one night he wasn't there. In the middle of recording a song, Barbra broke into tears. "She began to cry," a musician present told Shaun Considine, "she got on the phone, begging Jon to forgive her. She couldn't sing if he wasn't there. She pleaded with him to come to her. And meanwhile we're sitting around, something like forty musicians, listening to all this. Barbra usually was *tough* at the studio, but this guy got to her, and eventually he appeared. The songs she sang that night were 'Make the Man Love Me,' 'Being at War with Each Other,' and 'All in Love is Fair.' Appropriate titles, I felt."

One who was not completely pleased with the success of Barbra's album was Ray Stark, who was only getting a piece of the soundtrack album. He threatened to sue, and Columbia had to change the title to *Barbra Streisand: The Way We Were.* Still, there was no hiding the news that it contained Barbra's latest hit single, "The Way We Were," and it soon went gold. So did the soundtrack album.

That November 2, *Barbra Streisand . . . and Other Musical Instruments,* her fifth network television special, aired on CBS. Reviews and ratings were lackluster. The chief complaint was that it was over the top: "The program is well-made, and it certainly is expensive. But it is overproduced, over-orchestrated and overbearing to the point of esthetic nausea," complained John O'Connor of the *New York Times.* On the other hand, Kay Gardella of the *New York Daily News* loved it: "Miss Streisand guides us through a musical journey that's as exciting as *Alice's Adventures in Wonderland.*

Indeed, you get curiouser and curiouser as this rhythmic, imaginative, and humorous hour unfolds, dominated, of course, by La Streisand, a consummate performer and brilliant architect of a stellar show business career." Despite lukewarm reviews and lackluster ratings, *Barbra Streisand . . . and Other Musical Instruments* would make a strong showing at the Emmys the following May. And CBS Records expected the television exposure to boost sales of her next album, trumpeting in a *Billboard* ad: "On Friday, November 2, forty million people previewed the new Barbra Streisand album."

When her exclusive contract with CBS expired in 1974 they did not renew. She was now committed to her career in movies and recording.

Her one-time admirer, Frank Rich, admitted that his affection for Barbra had faded at an accelerating pace, but he still found her intermittently exciting, "especially when she opens her mouth to sing, as in the movies of *Funny Girl* or *Hello, Dolly!* or even over the credits of *What's Up, Doc?*

"In *The Way We Were,* where she played the Marmelstein/Brice character in '30s radical drag, I found her affecting, funny, and even (in the bedroom scenes with Robert Redford) somewhat erotic."

"She is too totally honest and too candid for the world we live in, for the business she's in," Erlichman told Peter Evans of *Cosmopolitan* around that time. "I tell her, 'Barbra, make your interview like another scene. Have your big interview scene. I'll give you the right dialogue and attitudes and you can rehearse it like another role.' But she can't fake."

Although Erlichman was still representing Barbra, Jon was exerting more and more influence on her work. Barbra told Peter Evans: "I feel terribly guilty having to work. He doesn't want to be around when I'm working—and I don't want him to be because my concentration goes right out the window